Widely regarded as bei
tion of Ulster poets th
Michael Longley, JOHI
development of art ar
throughout his life. H
educated at Methodist ~~~~~~~
University Belfast. Between 1948 and 1972 he published
two collections and six pamphlets of poetry. From 1930
to 1957 he worked in the Belfast Museum and Art
Gallery, after which he became art director of the
Herbert Art Gallery and Museum in Coventry. On his
retirement in 1972 he returned to Belfast, where he died
in 1987. His last years were remarkably productive, see-
ing the publication of seven collections and two pam-
phlets of poetry, as well as one book and two mono-
graphs on art. *Rhyming Weavers*, his study of the country
poets of Antrim and Down, was published in 1974.

Rhyming Weavers

& other country poets
of Antrim and Down

edited by
JOHN HEWITT

foreword by
TOM PAULIN

THE
BLACKSTAFF
PRESS
BELFAST

First published in 1974 by
Blackstaff Press

This edition published in 2004 by Blackstaff Press
4c Heron Wharf, Sydenham Business Park
Belfast BT3 9LE, Northern Ireland
with the assistance of
the Arts Council of Northern Ireland
and the Ulster-Scots Agency

© Text, the estate of John Hewitt, 2004
© Foreword, Tom Paulin, 2004
All rights reserved

Typeset by Techniset Typesetters, Newton-le-Willows, Merseyside

Printed in Great Britain by Cox & Wyman

A CIP catalogue record for this book
is available from the British Library

ISBN 0-85640-757-7

www.blackstaffpress.com

CONTENTS

DEDICATION OF
'THE RHYMING WEAVERS'

for G. Brendan Adams,
Honorary Archivist of the Ulster Folk Museum

None in our day has to such sure effect
defined the textures of our tangled speech;
from barony and borough drawing each
well-handsel'd thread, that we may learn respect
for the rich colours of each dialect;
this, given ready usage, yet might teach
our tense minds to unclench, and, open, reach
across the gap that sunders sect from sect.

So take this tapestry of prose and rhyme,
the prose is mostly mine, the rhymes belong
to weaver, ploughman, blacksmith, from that time
before the schoolhouse tamed their lively tongue,
when spinning wheel and loom were at their prime
and every townland earned its name in song.

JOHN HEWITT

FOREWORD

John Hewitt published *Rhyming Weavers* in 1974, one of the very worst years of the Troubles. Reading it with keen attention when it came out, I noticed that the Ulster vernacular in which most of the poems were written chimed with a distinctive strand in the language of Seamus Heaney's third collection of poetry, *Wintering Out*. Published just over a year before Hewitt's anthology, Heaney's volume opens with a poem entitled 'Fodder', which begins:

> Or as we said,
> *fother*

Like Heaney, the Ulster poets Hewitt studied and anthologised offer similarly mixed registers, as they move between a sometimes perfect, melodious Augustan language – the polite language of printed texts – and the intimacy of the spoken vernacular. This recurrence to the vernacular in Hewitt and Heaney is one expression of the political crisis in the North – both poets are using local speech to define a distinctive Ulster identity.

This tension between polite and vernacular language in the poetry of the *Rhyming Weavers* is evident in a stanza from 'To the Reverend TT' that has stayed with me since I first read Hewitt's anthology all those years back:

> Among the rest that me attracts
> There's one of which I hear great cracks
> An' that's the *Elegant Extracts*.
>   So if ye hae it,
> Your humble rhymer Sir, expects
>   Or hopes ye'll gi'e it.

Here, Hugh Porter, the County Down weaver poet, is writing a verse epistle to his patron, and, as Hewitt points out in his extended introduction, is making play with the rather pretentious title the Reverend Vicesimus Knox gave to his anthology, *Elegant Extracts in Poetry Selected for the Improvement of Young Persons*. That vocal, convivial phrase 'great cracks' puts a witty accent on *Extracts* and claims it as native – *Extracks*. This in turn makes 'your humble rhymer Sir' wittily egalitarian – mock-formal – in the best Burnsian manner. These are poets who know how to move in and out of a douce, polite voice and when to assume a tender, intimate voice, which, as I say, is convivial. This witty social voice is central to radical Dissenting culture, as the example of Burns demonstrates. Unitarian thinkers praised it as 'sociality', and it rings through the verse letters these poets wrote. They delight in rhyming 'matter' with 'water', because 'watter' is how they hear and pronounce the word. They are also cosmopolitan, like the friend of Hugh Porter in 'Hospitality',

> wha cross'd the ocean wide,
> An' brought us owre fu' cantie,
> Upon a smooth castalian tide,
> Th' Italic *Homer, Dante*.

That rhyme, 'cantie' with 'Dante', is cheerfully clever, and it is meant to roughen the 'smooth castalian tide' with what Dante, speaking of a particular type of Tuscan dialect, termed the 'yrsuta', which can be loosely translated as the 'shaggy'. We see a similar interest in rough-textured language in Samuel Thompson's 'To a Hedgehog', published just after the 1798 uprising:

> Gudefaith thou disna want for pikes
> Baith sharp and rauckle;

> Thou looks (Lord save's) array'd in spikes
> A creepin' heckle.

A 'heckle' is a board with spikes for dressing flax, while 'rauckle' means 'strong' – both words are more than shaggy, they are prickly and abrasive.

What rings through the poems in *Rhyming Weavers* is the clatter and noise of manual labour, its controlling and enabling rhythms, its tools and materials:

> The cobbler soon was at the wark
> The aul' shoon quickly aff were toss'd;
> Quick they were clean'd and on the last;
> And on the knee were firmly placed,
> An' ticht the stirrup ower them laced:
> Wi' every clink the aul' hook's dirl -
> A' roun' like shot the tacks did birl -
> The ancient knife no raspin' sharps,
> An' through the ox hide wheezelin' starts;
> And now the elson eddyin' bores,
> While sturdy 'rist wi' tradesman's sough
> Weel nedds't thegether wi' a pegh.

The dissonant music of the cobbler at work is relished in these lines from Robert Huddleston's 'The Cobbler', as it is in one of my favourite moments from another of his poems, 'The Lammas Fair (Belfast)':

> There sits a tinker wi' his tins,
> A turner wi' his ladles;
> A gleg tongu'd spunkie's cryin' spoons,
> Anither's at her fables.

Looking up 'gleg' in C.I. Macafee's *A Concise Ulster Dictionary* I find it means 'sharp, keen, quick-witted, fluent in speech' and comes from the Old Norse 'glegger', meaning 'sharp-sighted, clever'. The word 'spunkie', from the Scottish Gaelic '*spong*, earlier *sponc* "tinder"', is a noun meaning, I would guess, 'an energetic character'. Macafee's *Concise Ulster Dictionary* and James Fenton's dictionary of Ulster Scots, *The Hamely Tongue*, were both published more than twenty years after the publication of *Rhyming Weavers*. Both dictionaries must in part have been inspired by John Hewitt's work, and also by the many volumes of poetry published by Northern Irish writers over the last decades. In this context it is worth mentioning an important work that predates *Rhyming Weavers* by ten years. *Ulster Dialect: An Introductory Symposium* was published in 1964 by the Ulster Folk Museum and can be seen as representing a new, optimistic confidence in the future of the province at that time. It was edited by G.B. Adams, to whom Hewitt dedicates *Rhyming Weavers*.

The weaver poets record and preserve not just local words, but also the customs, textures and cadences of rural life. In these lines from Huddleston's 'Creevy Hall', younger readers will find a sound recorded which has now almost vanished from the island as a result of mechanised farming:

> The eve got dusk, the wind was still,
>> The Corncraik turned her haverl lyre,
> And far away o'er Seefar-Hill,
>> The Cuckoo's chorus joined the choir;
> The thrush sang drowsy day to rest,
>> In Anderson's lone sylvan shaw;
> And onward, as I homeward passed,
>> The Redbreast sung by Creevy Ha'.

The word 'haverl' here means 'coarse, awkward, annoying', with the idea of 'talkative nonsense' thrown in. The lines beautifully mix the cadence of Ulster speech and dialect – 'The eve got dusk' – with poetic diction – 'lone sylvan'. The monotony of the corncrake's song, day and night, is caught in that intriguing phrase 'haverl lyre', and the result is a perfectly pitched stanza.

Thomas Given's 'A Song for February', which inspired me more than twenty years ago to try a similar subject, is confident in its vernacular:

> The blackbird keeks out frae the fog at the broo,
> Gees his neb a bit dicht on a stane;

The blackbird jumps out of the long stems of last year's grass on the brow of a ditch – the observation has a lithe naturalness, which is confident and unaffected as speech. To read these poems is to drink at the well of a plain-spoken, witty, confident and egalitarian culture, and an at times nonchalant intelligence, which draws on texts and language belonging to polite culture in order to affirm and explore an imaginative idea that exists beyond the simple, binary division between polite language and dialect, the polished and the shaggy.

In a recent poem, 'To George Seferis in the Underworld', Seamus Heaney takes the dialect word 'seggan', given to various species of reeds, rushes and sedges, and identifies it with 'asphodel'. He then speaks of getting

> a chance to test the edge
> of a word like *seggans*, smuggle it back in
> like a dialect blade, hoar and harder
> than what it has turned into
> these latter days:
> sedge, marshmallow, rubber-dagger stuff.

The dialect poets in Hewitt's *Rhyming Weavers*, like George Seferis, belong among the shades. They are significant figures in the Ulster Enlightenment, whose poems should be cherished and explored and cited. John Hewitt's anthology, re-issued here, initiated a process of cultural recovery and restitution which needs to be constantly recognised and encouraged.

TOM PAULIN
April 2004

PREFACE

The title of this book fairly indicates its nature and scope. The volumes of verse examined may be found in the Kennedy and the Belfast Printed Books Collections in the Linen Hall Library, Belfast, in the Bigger Collection in the Belfast Public Library, and on my own much shorter shelves.

Of the background material it would be cumbersome and ploddingly pedantic to list every item. Many of the books and journals are mentioned in the text. For the rest, D.J. O'Donoghue's *The Poets of Ireland: A Biographical and Bibliographical Dictionary of Irish Writers of English Verse* (1912), has been my base and foundation. J. Anderson's *Catalogue of Early Belfast Printed Books* with its supplements, provided important dates. Scottish references were based on T.F. Henderson's *Scottish Vernacular Literature* (3rd revised edition, 1910), David Daiches' *Robert Burns* (1951) and *A Scots Anthology from the Thirteenth to the Twentieth Century*, edited by John W. Oliver and J.C. Smith (1949).

I have also drawn upon or modified passages which I had previously written, from such sources as:

1 'Ulster Poets 1800–1850', a paper read to the Belfast Literary Society, 3 January 1951, which was subsequently printed for private distribution;

2 'The Rhyming Weavers', three articles in *Fibres, Fabrics and Cordage*, vol. 15, nos 7, 8 and 9 (1948);

3 'The Course of Writing in Ulster' in *Rann,* no. 20 (June 1953);

4 and from my own unpublished thesis, *Ulster Poets 1800–1870* (1951).

My introduction to this last ended with the sentence: 'But I could not have read so many thousand lines if the forgotten and often clumsy old poets themselves had not now and then given me, in stanza, couplet or turn of phrase, some sense of the humanity that was in them, and some feeling that, for better or worse, they were my own people . . .' And, after twenty years, with my recent and, I hope, better informed re-reading, that judgement stands.

1974

The
SUBJECT
PROPOSED

One aspect of the literary life of the eighteenth century in these islands not often discussed nowadays was the fashionable urge to offer patronage to the uneducated working-class author. From Stephen Duck of *The Thresher's Labour* to Robert Bloomfield of *The Farmer's Boy*, the names crowd in; Robert Tatersal, the Kingston bricklayer; James Woodhouse, the Rowley cobbler; Ann Yearsley, the Bristol milkwoman; James Frederick Bryant, pipe-maker of the same town; Henry Nelson, the Dublin bricklayer . . .

But it was the fame of the Ayrshire ploughman, Robert Burns, which established the archetypal figure in the general imagination, although in effect, he stood outside the convention of 'the unlettered bard', drawing as he did upon long established technical usages of a strong national tradition, the tradition of Scottish vernacular literature which had received renewed impetus in the revivalism of Allan Ramsay early in the century, and had been given a contemporary vigour in the work of Robert Fergusson. And it was the idea of the peasant poet as an acceptable role, which certainly inspired many country folk to try their hands at the making of verses, since there seemed to be a reservoir of goodwill for the intention and support for the effort among the educated classes.

But that is only part of our story. In the province of Ulster, colonised to varying degrees of thoroughness in the seventeenth century, from the middle of the succeeding century, the wars of occupation well past, and the colony firmly rooted, there was a period of surprising poetic activity on many levels – landed gentry, gentlewomen, clergymen of the established church, schoolmasters, students, journalists, as well as peasants and rural craftsmen. The well-off had their volumes printed in London and Dublin, and, because of their styles of verse and the audiences they had in mind, I find it useful to group them under the name of *Colonial*; like the writers of New England, the Cape Colony and New South Wales. A second category, which appeared a little later, were those who had in mind a more local audience and paid less attention to metropolitan conventions or fashions, and were bourgeois or petit-bourgeois in origin and usually townsmen. These I designate as *Provincial*. For the peasants and rural craftsmen, I reserve the title, *Vernacular*, since their written idiom was largely that of the words which they spoke, not the language of print.

The most thoroughly colonised parts of Ulster had been inhabited by Scots brought over in large numbers to north Down by the Ayrshire lairds, Hamilton and Montgomery, and to mid-Antrim by the Earl of Antrim, before the King's plantation of mid-Ulster, and about the same time as the filling of the Lagan valley with English settlers introduced by Chichester. So the language of the colonists in Antrim and Down was the central Scots of the western Lowlands, later to be subject to varying degrees of modification and dilution, touching, as it did, upon the wedge of English and the mountainous country of south Down and the Glens of Antrim, where the older inhabitants still had foothold. That there was a high degree of literacy among the Scots population may be gauged from the circumstance that Allan Ramsay's popular *Gentle Shepherd* was printed in Belfast as early as 1748 and had a number of subsequent editions; that the first book to be printed in Newry in 1760 was the same work; that Sir David Lindsay's *Poems* had come from a Belfast press in 1714; and Alexander Montgomerie's *The Cherry and the Slae*, with its highly sophisticated stanza, from the same town in 1731. That there was a local demand for these classics of Scots literature long before Burns began to write helps to give scale and perspective to his later popularity and influence.

Oddly enough, the first printed verses by a local author in Scots figure in a broadsheet from Strabane, about 1735, in the stanza sometimes called after Burns, but far older than his practice, and more accurately known as Standard Habbie, since it was fixed in the Scots prosody by Robert Sempill's *Life and Death of Habbie Simpson*, written in 1640 or thereabouts. A little later than the Strabane broadsheet, our first anthology of prose and verse, *The Ulster Miscellany* (1753) has a section of seventeen pages under the heading of Scotch Poems, several of which specifically relate to the Scots-planted pocket in east Donegal. Among the more interesting of these, a pastoral nightpiece presents accurate local description:

> The night is pleasant, lown and clear,
> Ye'll see the muntins far and near,
> Ald Doowish wi' his lowtin' beck
> Ald Muckish like a long peat stack.

This poem also established domestic detail which will prove familiar throughout our period:

> Fye, woman, quat the purrin' wheel
> And gi' the wench her pirn to reel
> Ye've deen, or else the sorrow's in't,
> Ye've caust yere hank, and that's the stint.

There is also a pastoral elegy on the death of Jonathan Swift, DD, late DSPD – the last splay of initials must stand for 'Dean of St Patrick's Dublin'. Many of the couplets are rigidly in the mould of the particular convention:

> He was the blythest shepherd e'er was seen,
> The King o' mirth, the wonder o' the green.

But the reference to the episode of Wood's Halfpence, the agitation against which marked Swift's identification with the people of his native land, has a dense linguistic texture, far from standard English:

> As elves, they say, the thriving bairnie nick,
> And lie' a crowl in lieu, or rotten stick.

It can be asserted then with some confidence, that because of climatic similarity, the Scots planters were able to resume and continue an economic and social pattern of life almost identical with that of their original homeland, that they carried with them unaltered the manual skills and habits of thought and expression, their respect for books, their presbyterian form of Protestantism, and because they had come into a context where feudalism had never been the order, they were able, by usage though not by law, to achieve a tenure of their holdings more liberal than that which they had left.

As I have said, the colonies were planted with differing degrees of thoroughness. There were no fences or frontiers between the Scots and the English. The native Irish landowners were mostly dispossessed, but their clansmen, their tenants, in many instances were allowed to remain as labourers for new masters. The north-east coast of Antrim was still occupied by the Gaels of the Western Isles. And to the west and north-west, save in a few enclaves like that of the Scots in Donegal, the Irish far outnumbered the newcomers who tended to be those who had received vast tracts of land. Only the north Down and mid-Antrim areas of Scots settlement showed any extreme preponderance of colonists over the indigenous folk. This meant that there was inevitably a linguistic intermixture. As Hugh Porter of Moneyslan, County Down, indicates (1813):

> – in the style appears
> The accent o' my early years,
> Which is nor Scotch or English either,
> But part o' both mix'd up thegither;
> Yet is the sort my neighbours use
> Who think shoon prettier than shoes . . .

Social pressures were apparent. James Orr of Ballycarry in his 'The Irish Cottier's Death and Burial' recalls how, when the minister came in, the mourners tried

> To quate braid Scotch, a task that foils their art.

In this connexion, it is worth remembering that in the Scottish Universities the vernacular was despised. Francis Hutcheson, the eminent philosopher, himself a County Down man, had established 'the more educated' usages as obligatory, and when Presbyterian ministers of the

North of Ireland came back from the crosswater col-
leges, they made scarcely any impact on the writing of
verse in the old tongue. The difference between these
and clergymen of the established church, who had tradi-
tionally been educated at Trinity College Dublin or, in
some instances, at Oxford and Cambridge, is most
marked, for among the latter were such poets as the
Reverend Henry E. 'Dante' Boyd, the Reverend Samuel
Burdy, William Carr and, outside our period, William
Alexander, Archbishop of Armagh, as well as others born
elsewhere but later resident in the province, like Bishop
Richard Mant and Dean Daniel Bagot.

It was recognised that Scots was the sinew of the local
speech. Samuel Ferguson, writing to a northern friend
regarding a verse epistle in Standard Habbie (1885),
remarked 'so say I in our native Doric, forty years ago'.
James McKowen, the Bard of Lambeg, in a note to
Ralph Varian the anthologist (1869) wrote 'There is a
kind of Scotch dialect spoken in these parts of Co.
Antrim'. Mrs Alexander, wife of the Archbishop, still
remembered for her hymns, in a note on her fine Ulster
ballad, 'The Legend of Stumpie's Brae', used the phrase
'the peculiar semi-Scottish dialect spoken in the North
of Ireland', and Charles K. Pooler, a fine balladist himself,
described his *Idylls of Ulster* (1900) as written in 'the very
variable dialect, once Scotch, now spoken in parts of
Ireland'. Neither Pooler nor Mrs Alexander can be con-
sidered as belonging to the Vernacular category. For
testimony from that side we may quote Thomas Beggs in
the preface to the *Second Part of the Minstrel's Offering*
(1836): 'Should the reader of the following effusions sup-
pose that in some parts the author has imitated the
Scottish dialect, – he would wish to correct the idea,
by alleging that he has written in his own style in the

language of his native glen – not constrained, but spontaneous as the lispings of our first speech.' And the sturdy Robert Huddleston (1844) declares that he uses 'the language which nature brought him to his door, and handed to him at the first dawn of prattle, and bade him wear through life'.

This was their own language, not a borrowed garb, the trappings of imitated compositions. One characteristic detail in the verses is that often, particularly with those bards who handled a dense idiom, the rhymes are approximate, vowel-rhymes or assonances, more usually. I take this to be of the nature of verse 'made-up in the head' before it is put on paper; the ear more readily than the eye is satisfied with such effects. So too assonance is something of an old device in the Border Ballads which travelled orally for a long time till they found their broadsheets. And it would not be rash to suggest that versing at the loom was in a measure responsible. James Campbell of Ballynure customarily 'kept an inkhorn and paper within reach', for 'the principal part of his stanzas was composed at the loom . . .' I also believe that if the printed verses seem, on the page, to be in something near to standard English in spelling, we should listen carefully with the mind's ear for the vernacular cadence and pronunciation.

From this it is clear that the full canon of Scots was seldom evoked, and became less and less called upon with the passing years, for a living language is a changing language.

It has been the uncritical custom of our older bookmen and antiquarians, who give little evidence of having looked into the books with any care, to assert that the entire activity in the vernacular was derived from the widely popular example of Robert Burns. One of these, writing as recently as 1959, of Alexander McKenzie, describes him as 'one of the last of imitators', when a careful study of the texts would have shown that in his volume of 130 pages of verse, only one poem is 'in the Scottish dialect', and that, actually, a lyric lightly tinctured with it, that McKenzie by the evidence of the notes he appended, owed more to William Falconer of *The Shipwreck* than to any other poet of his reading; a reviewer, in 1810, suggested that he leaned too heavily on Thomas Gray.

It would be wilfully rushing to extremes to deny that any influence operated. Burns' *Poems* were printed in Belfast several times before his death, once in the same year of the first Edinburgh edition (1787). Certainly the local bards made verses on similar subjects to the master. Both Burns' 'Cotter's Saturday Night' and Orr's 'The Irish Cottier's Death and Burial' were composed in Spenserian stanzas, but if we accept John Spiers' judgement in his *Scots Literary Tradition* (1940) that the former is an obvious 'fake' in idiom and feeling, an honest estimate might be offered that *in this instance* Orr was the better folk-poet. Francis Boyle wrote 'The Author's Address' to his old gelding based on Burns' 'The Auld Farmer's Salutation to his Auld Mare', but he clearly had a gelding and not a mare in his mind's eye.

Samuel Thomson of Carngranny went to visit Burns in the spring of 1794 and five years later published a blank verse poem on the event:

O Yes, Hibernians, I beheld the Bard.

Luke Mullan, brother-in-law of the well-known James Hope, the United Irishman, and a member of the Four Towns Book Club, 'had the pleasure of being introduced to the bard', and when Burns died, there were sheaves of elegies, such as those by Orr and Boyle, to signalise their respect and grief.

Burns had, as I have said, taken Standard Habbie from Ramsay and Fergusson: so too *The Holy Fair* stanza had come to him from the latter's 'Leith-Races'; this, developed from *Christ's Kirk on the Green*, traditionally ascribed to James V, had been used by Alexander Scott and others until taken up by Ramsay. It would seem that if borrowing technical devices be the test, it would be fair to suggest that the Ulster Vernacular bards were in much the same relationship to Burns as he had been to his predecessors, and were working free-handedly within the same tradition; and as Burns took without any sense of plagiarism, stanzas, lines, themes, from the vernacular literature of his folk, so the Ulster bards should not be faulted for following the practice. The most popular stanza had, as I have shown, a footing in Ulster before Burns' birth: the other great stanzas were traditional; and if Burns showed how these might be used to best effect, were they to decline his tutelage? Anyhow, as I have noted, they were already in locally printed books. Frank Boyle, in his book of 1811, declares that he was over eighty years of age, and had been writing verse for at least forty of them; that means when Burns was only eleven or twelve, before his poetry began.

THE PUBLICATION
of the
LITTLE BOOKS

These little books, stitched paper or in boards, which are the bards' memorials and the substance of this study, were for the most part printed in Belfast. Some of the country writers outside Antrim or Down found printers nearer home, in such places as Portadown, Dungannon, Enniskillen, Strabane; but, for those we are concerned with it was Alexander Mackay of the *Belfast Newsletter*, Simms and McIntyre, Smith and Lyons, F.D. Finlay of the *Northern Whig*, Joseph Smyth, Hugh Clarke, and James Reed who put print upon the poets' lines. There were three exceptions. John McKinley brought out a second revised edition of his *Poetic Sketches descriptive of the Giant's Causeway and the Surrounding Scenery: with some Detached Pieces* (1821) in Dublin, two years after Joseph Smyth had published the first in Belfast. Much later in the century Samuel Corry of Ballyclare brought out on his own press there *The Poetical Works of Thomas Beggs* (1867) and in 1870, *The Poems and Songs of James Campbell of Ballynure with additional songs not before published*.

The business of publication was financed by subscriptions, friends, acquaintances or prestigious persons being solicited to take one or more copies of the book when printed, at a stated figure, usually half a crown. This method applied not merely to the country bards but to any poet who was unable himself to pay the printer. James McHenry, later to become a popular novelist, prefaced his first book with the remark that he had 'determined after some deliberation, to risk the publication of a few of [his] pieces. This [he] was necessitated to do by subscription, because [his] inclination constrained [him] to publish in [his] own country, where it is to be lamented, there is no other mode of publication that affords any prospect of success'.

It was the custom, after the successful circulation of a preliminary prospectus, to print, in the first or last pages of the volume, a list of the subscribers' names, and if any took more than one copy the number was given. The most successful venture in this was Alexander McKenzie's *Poems and Songs* (1810) which, published for 3s 6d, netted the author £200 from over two thousand subscribers. With this remarkable sum – Robert Burns with three hundred subscribers for his Kilmarnock edition (1786), and a printing of six hundred copies sold at three shillings, 'after deducting all expenses' pocketed, according to his own account, 'nearly £20' – McKenzie built himself a cottage which he named 'Mount Gaelus' to celebrate the pseudonym he used for his contributions to the *Newsletter*. He also bought a fishing boat. This was wrecked, McKenzie nearly drowned, and, as he had omitted to obtain any security for the funds he had lodged with the local land agent, he found himself evicted about 1812.

The only other volumes to pass the one thousand subscribers among our bards were John McKinley's *Giant's Causeway* (1819) and his second Dublin edition (1821) and *The Rude Rhymes* (1824) of Bernard Short, the very bad Armagh poetaster. So far as we can estimate from the lists, most other volumes of this kind only attracted a few hundred subscribers each.

These lists have an importance beyond the merely statistical. From them it is often possible to deduce a great deal about the writer; how far his appeal extended; through what levels of society; in some circumstances, what his political leanings were; or his religious affiliation; and something of his social interests; as, for instance whether he could be presumed to have been a Freemason.

McKenzie's list, for example, is drawn largely from the Ards peninsula and the rest of County Down, but contains 144 names of Scottish subscribers. Thomas Percy, Bishop of Dromore, in the North of Ireland, a generous patron of the poets, and a useful name to have on your list, took three copies; but his interest did not end there. His son-in-law, the Honourable and Reverend P. Meade; his aristocratic friend Edward Ward; his chaplain, the Reverend Henry E. Boyd; the Reverend William Hamilton Drummond; Thomas Stott, the Dromore bleacher-poet savaged by Byron; and the Reverend William Neilson, the scholar in Irish, were all members of the Bishop's coterie. Archibald Rowan Hamilton appears more likely in his capacity as a County Down landowner than as a prominent figure in national politics. James McHenry of Larne and James Orr of Ballycarry show approbation of a fellow poet, and, besides, McHenry was just then cultivating the Dromore circle. Robert Anderson, the Cumberland poet to whose own volume both Wordsworth and Southey had subscribed, and who was working at Carnmoney is also here, as he is in almost every other subscription list of the time. He very likely secured the six subscriptions from the Carnmoney Reading Society since he was its most eminent member. Another reading society, that of Crawfordsburn, is included. Among the verses in the book there is a set dedicated to the Green Hill Lodge, No. 985, and that body responded lavishly with fifty subscriptions. Another lodge, Cabra, No. 606, is credited with four. Noblemen, clergy, doctors pepper the roster, and names of persons of contemporary, if short-lived literary interest may be found, like Anne Lutton of Moira, once a celebrated Methodist lay preacher in England; Mrs Aeneas Lamont of Belfast, whose *Poems and Tales in Verse* was to be published in London in 1818; and William Anderson, the Saintfield schoolmaster and author of 'Moral poems'. A list of such length and complexity predicates a remarkable organisational skill in its assembling far beyond the scope of a poor hand-loom weaver in an Ards townland.

For Hugh Porter's *Poetical Attempts by Hugh Porter, a County of Down Weaver* (1813) it was the Reverend Thomas Tighe, close friend of the Reverend Henry Boyd, translator of Dante, and attached to the Dromore group, who activated the undertaking. This brought in seventy-seven clergy including five bishops, the representatives of twenty-two titled houses, and, surprisingly, fifteen Cambridge dons in its tally of almost seven hundred. Bishop Percy is credited posthumously with four copies; Boyd of course, Drummond, and Dr James McDonnell, the celebrated Belfast surgeon, lend the authority of their reputations 'to exhilarate the evening of the author's life by raising a little fund for that purpose', as the Apologetical Address to the Reader phrases it.

By contrast with those socially impressive musters, Orr's *Poems on Various Subjects* (1804) with under five hundred subscribers, is drawn from his own native townland of Broadisland, Ballycarry, from the adjacent Islandmagee, Larne and Carrickfergus, with only eighteen individuals from Belfast – the town's booksellers had more confidence and took one hundred copies. Magheramorne Book Club is listed for ten, but only Orr's brother – bard Sam Thomson of Carngranny and the radical John Hancock of Lisburn, friend of William Drennan, have any sort of significance in themselves.

The Posthumous Works of James Campbell of Ballynure (1820) had as its worthy purpose to raise funds for the widow and children, but it gathered no more than 246 listed names, Thomas Beggs the only bard. There are three Masonic lodges, and a single clergyman, a circumstance not surprising in view of James Campell's lively anti-clerical opinions. Again the majority is from the Ballynure–Ballyclare area.

By contrast with Campbell, John McKinley of Dunseverick is seen by the list in his *Giant's Causeway* (1819) to have commanded an amazingly dispersed audience – from Portrush to Portaferry, from Larne to Ballyshannon it ranges, with some emphasis on the north coast, to Antrim and Londonderry, the northern and western hinterlands of Lough Neagh, south Down and Belfast, which is certainly not the pattern for the localised bard. His literary standing is vouched for by Robert Anderson who was on the point of returning or had already returned to Carlisle; by 'Dante' Boyd; Drummond, now of Dublin; Thomas Stott; James McHenry; the spinster Mary Balfour of Limavady; Thomas Beggs; and Alexander McKenzie still described as 'of Dunover', although he had been living in Belfast for about six years. W.H. Maxwell, future author of *The Wild Sports of the West*, and J. Sheridan Knowles 'of Glasgow', the playwright who taught school in

Belfast for some years, bring to mind once popular names. Dr James McDonnell and the Reverend William Bruce, headmaster of the Belfast Academy, suggest the nature of the town's support, reinforced by 'Mr J. Emerson' who was most probably the future Sir James Emerson Tennent, politician and dedicatee of Dickens' *Our Mutual Friend*, shortly to be involved in the Greek War of Independence. Six Masonic lodges are noted, from Dervock to Greyabbey, and a reading society, that of Bangor. Also from County Down, the Reverend Thomas Tighe of Drumgooland, patron of Hugh Porter. An unusual muster of Irish surnames like O'Hanlon, O'Flinn, O'Cain, O'Raw, O'Dougherty might suggest that McKinley had some Roman Catholic association, an interesting fact borne out by the number of subscriptions from Maynooth drawn by his second Dublin edition (1821) which seems to have crossed sectarian lines with some vigour.

Even this cursory glance reveals the value of these lists in helping the historian to appreciate the cross-currents and meshing in the social fabric of the period. It certainly indicates that in the earlier years of the last century the poet had some claim to prestige and status in his community.

Although not starred with distinguished names, the list given in John Dickey's *Poems on Various Subjects* of 1818, while numbering a little over two hundred, is unique in its kind. It is set out as:

Subscribers names/poetically and alphabetically arranged/and in due order we have them rhymed for us in couplets, with the prelude: –

With soul-thrilling pleasure, ye warm-hearted few,
Whose names on my list of subscribers I view,

Your names and your surnames and names of
   your places,
My rude, rustic muse, with all diligence traces.

A

The noble 'squire Henry Adair, Loughamore,
And Thomas Agnew too, of old Donegore . . .

B

John Burns, Templepatrick, John Barr of Kilbride,
Tom Beggs, Ballyclare, who in singing takes pride . . .

C

The Rev'rend, the kind Henry Cooke, Killeleagh,
(Two copies will take) once my pastor and stay
John Courtney of Doagh, is no pitiful scrub;
Two copies are ta'en by Carngranny Book Club.

G

John Getty, of Randlestown, listens my strain,
And Reverend Priest Gribben of Magheralane.

H

Anne Harbison, Rockfield, is meaning to pore
Some nights on my book, when her spinning
   is o'er . . .

Mc

In gay Donegore John McMullen will be
With poet McKinley of Dervock for me.
Alexander McTrusty is one of the throng
That give half a crown in exchange for my song . . .

Tom Beggs is, of course, the indefatigable subscriber,
always eager to demonstrate his craft solidarity. Henry

Cooke (1788–1857) had been Presbyterian minister of Donegore from 1810 to 1818, and was later to become a figure in national controversy. John Getty is very likely the mid-Antrim schoolmaster versifier, and poet McKinley received Dickey's support for his own volume in the following year. The price of the book, half a crown, was the same as each of Robert Huddleston's in 1844 and 1846. The bulk of subscribers came from Larne to the east, Antrim to the west, and Belfast to the south, concentrated in the valley of the Six Mile Water, the Donegore, Doagh, Templepatrick district, very much the territory of the south Antrim bards, Orr, Campbell, Beggs, Samuel Walker; there, if ever, is the local bard on his own home-ground and not reaching much beyond it.

This was the very area defined in Samuel Ferguson's essay, 'Attractions of Ireland, No. 3' (*Dublin University Magazine*, December 1836): 'Robert Burns' own parish was not more deeply imbued with the love of song than the central district of the county of Antrim. We could enumerate at least a dozen rustic poets whose works have been published from time to time in a district not more than fifteen miles in length by ten in breadth.'

He then reviews, not unfavourably, with copious quotations, 'the last volume which emanated from his little rustic Arcadia', *Feudal Scenes* (Belfast 1833) by John Fullarton. Fullarton (1806–1875) was certainly a native of that little rustic Arcadia, living in Ballynure where he had been born, until he left to work for a Belfast engineer and millwright in 1843. Friend of many of the bards – David Herbison called him 'one of the earliest, truest and kindest friends'. I possess his autographed copy of *Midnight Musings; or Thoughts from the Loom* (1848), one of the two copies for which he is entered on the subscribers list – he wrote short biographies of half a dozen northern poets for the *Ulster Magazine*. But his verse never was vernacular, dealing instead with the themes 'of Chivalry and Feudalism' in a dull if correct English. His one Irish narrative, *O'More, A Tale of War* (1867), runs to over two thousand lines in the Spenserian stanza. As he tells us in his interesting 'Recollections' prefacing the volume, the two books which followed *Feudal Scenes* were published at his own expense, for 'in a pecuniary point of view, the publication of my first volume profited me nothing, and I thence concluded that another work would be attended with no better success'. Ferguson considered that the book was 'very creditable to the author, and still more to the district'. Even more relevant to our purpose, he mentions that it had been published by subscription at 3s 6d per copy and that 'the names of the subscribers amount to one hundred and fifty three, of *these three only are above the rank of the small farmer;* the bulk of the subscribers to this volume of poems having considerable epic pretentions are weavers and cotiers'.

Just over a quarter of a century earlier, an anonymous reviewer, discussing Alexander McKenzie's book in the *Belfast Monthly Magazine*, was critical of the ostentatious length of his subscribers list, but felt impelled to commend a large number of names drawn from the farmers and rural workers of the Ards, evidencing the rise in cultural standards in the province.

Ferguson refers to a further example of this phenomenon: 'Another volume of poems published under not much higher patronage was the production of a humble weaver of Donegore; they are chiefly in the Scottish dialect, and possess, in the midst of all sorts of bad taste, both humour and pathos.' This is, very likely, John

Dickey's book which could have come to his attention when Ferguson was a boy. For, although he was born in Belfast in 1810, that was in the house of his maternal grandparents, and his father's father had 'a good estate around and including the little town of Parkgate . . . in and about the valley of the Six Mile Water'. This had come to the Fergusons in the mid-seventeenth century, and was in process of being dispersed by the unthrifty habits of the sons of 'Samuel Ferguson of Standing Stone in the County of Antrim', but grandson Samuel was able to spend much of his boyhood and youth on various fragments of it.

Among Dickey's subscribers we find that 'William Ferguson Esquire of Thrushfield' took two copies, and 'Miss Mary and Miss Betty (Ferguson) will each take a book', and

From College James Ferguson sends for my lays.

To this William Ferguson Dickey inscribed his Address to Parkgate. In Lady Ferguson's biography of her husband there is a reference to 'the Fergusons of Thrushfield, from whom is descended Sir Samuel Ferguson of Dublin'. Place, name and class are consistent. These were his kinsfolk; the ladies may have been his sisters, William can hardly have been his eldest brother, that William who was killed in 1828 serving under Bolivar in the South American War of Independence. James was likely a cousin.

Samuel Ferguson's recollection of the book as 'chiefly in the Scottish dialect', is slightly at fault; only about a third of the verses are in the vernacular; and most of these are only very lightly so, as are the stanzas in which the bard accepts the necessity of seeking subscriptions:

I recognise your friendly hint,
O' telling me that I should print;
I fear there's naething in my mint,
  I dare advance
But I'll put on a face o' flint
  And tak my chance.

Nae patronising shield have I,
To which I may for shelter fly,
And crouch while storms may brattle by,
  Secure frae harm
Where I might hear the carping fry
  Without alarm.

No! I, let weal or woe betide,
The brunt o'every storm maun bide;
I'll never knuckle down to pride,
  To count a patron;
In my subscribers I'll confide
  Which is nae flatt'rin!

Treating the subscribers' names as interesting items in themselves, we have failed to consider seriously the tedious work which must have been endured in assembling them. There is evidence that after the preliminary prospectus had been sent out, the actual canvassing would have been done by the expectant poet himself. For this we have a few stanzas from Hugh McWilliams' *Poems and Songs* (1831):

To publish what the muse has spun,
To get subscribers, I hae run
'Mongst my acquaintance, scarcely one
  In ten refused:

> But where I am unkent, alone,
>   I'm coldly used ...
>
> Some tell me they hae books that they
> Scarce ever open – others say
> They hae nae taste for poetry
>   An' seem unwilling,
> While many, with alacrity,
>   Hand out the shilling ...
>
> While I a district hae surveyed,
> And few or no subscribers made,
> I feel confoundedly dismayed;
>   Without disguising,
> I'm inclined to quit the trade
>   Of poetizing.

This book gives no list, but from the author's preface we learn that he lived at Loughgeel, north Antrim, and that his canvassing took him as far as County Down where he had kept a school in earlier years.

That the bard on occasion was not required to work single-handedly we discover from a moving sentence in Robert Huddleston's *A Collection of Poems and Songs on Rural Subjects* (1844), prefacing his list of almost four hundred, largely drawn from the north Down area and Belfast and containing not a single otherwise noteworthy name. He offers his thanks 'to those who have taken upon themselves the trouble of canvassing (and the reader will find them in italics)'; 'he leaves them and the brave folks of their gathering, their names along with his own, with the hope that they will survive, when he and they shall be no more'.

And sure enough there they are: 'Richard Galbraith, Belfast; M.J. Fisher, Moneyrea; Doctor McMurray,

Killinchy; William Stewart, Saktric Castle; John Macoubry, Tullygirvan; John Pettigrew, Tullygirvan; Thomas Neilson, Castlespie . . .' Less than shadows now, they once gave practical help to their poet and he hoped that they would be remembered for it.

A NOTE
on reading
THE BARDS' VERSES

When these books of the bards were printed there was seldom thought of supplying glossaries of unfamiliar words, for the words were familiar to their readers, written as their own native language sounded, Scots speckled with a few Irish words.

There was no general rule about spelling; there had not been, even in English, for centuries – you remember the old joke about Shakespeare not knowing how to spell his own name.

As Tom Scott, that fine poet, writes in his trenchant introduction to *The Penguin Book of Scottish Verse* (1970): 'We today live in a world in which spelling correctly is taken for granted. It never occurs to most of us that there is no such thing as "correct" spelling, and that obsessive neurosis, imposed on us by teachers at school, was originally imposed on teachers, and on all society, by ignorant printers who couldn't spell. They had to have everything reduced to an easy standard that they could learn.'

Further, of the old Scots poets, he writes, 'This nonsense was as unknown as the knowledge of good and evil

to Adam before the Fall. They spelt any old how, were
totally inconsistent, spelt how they heard, or thought, or
felt, and that only according to mood. You will find the
same word spelt several different ways in the same short
poem.'

This lack of consistency we find among the bards'
verses. 'With' will be spelt *wi'*, *we* or *wae*, with the added
confusion that *wae* also represents the word 'woe'. So that
the reader has to judge, without much difficulty, which
makes sense in a particular context.

A number of words once spoken in Antrim and
Down have gone out of use, have become forgotten, and
these need explanation, though seldom can these expla-
nations be exact, or represent all the shades of meaning.
Take the lines of Thomas Given of Cullybackey:

> The blackbird keeks out frae the fog at the broo,
> Gees his neb a bit dicht on a stane.

To keek means something more precise than simply 'to
look', 'to peep'. There is always a furtiveness about it.
With *oot frae* there should be no trouble. *The fog at the
broo* means roughly 'the long grass left standing after
winter' in the ditch at the side of the field. For the sec-
ond line, *Gees his neb* is fairly obviously 'Gives his beak'.
A bit dicht on a stane: dicht, Robert Burns used to spell this
word *dight*, means something more exact than 'to wipe';
it means rather a quick flick-of-a-wipe. My mother
always spoke of giving her nose a dicht of powder – *a bit
dicht* makes the flick even lighter. There aren't three
words in English which could catch that gesture. You
couldn't offer word for word translation.

Here we are touching upon the intractability of trans-
lation in verse. Unless we know the associations and

reverberations a word has to its native speakers we can only offer an approximation to its 'meaning'.

Take a few more lines, from John McKinley this time:

> The winsome matron at the wheel
> Wi' canny e'e keeks at the chiel
> She thinks wad fit her Jenny weel . . .

Matron here does not postulate an institution. It was the spinning wheel this country mother was at, not the wheel of a car. As she spins, she steals a quick, cautious, prudent, gentle glance or furtive look – the glossaries give authority to all these shades of meaning; 'To keek with canny eyes' gives that action a very particular quality, appropriate since she is looking at the fellow who, she fancies, would make a good husband for her daughter. Already in both instances twisting and pushing the sense of the words into English makes them leak and spill out of the brief lines of compact verse.

Sir George Douglas in his little book *Poems of the Scottish Minor Poets* (1891) writes that many of the Scottish words 'are in reality identical with the English equivalents, though somewhat differently spelt and pronounced, – *heid* for instance, for head; *braid* for broad and the like'. We could add *auld* for old, *sang* for song, *wha* for who, *hamely* for homely, *simmer* for summer, *weel* for well, *ane* for one, and so on. These should not set an intelligent reader an impossible task to understand.

So rather than pepper the margins of these pages with obvious or fairly obvious variant spellings of words familiar in English, only those words will be 'translated' which would be utterly strange and unguessable to a non-Scots reader.

For the rest, if the verses are read out loud, the ear will

prove to be better informed than the eye, for, as in all poetry, the sound and sense are inextricably bound together. As the late W.R. Rodgers used to say: it's a matter of *sound* sense and sound *sense*.

There was indeed one particular book with a two-page glossary, Henry McDonald Flecher's *Poems, Songs and Ballads* (1866). He had been a schoolmaster, and as well as authentic vernacular he used many Irish words, such as Aroon, Asthore, Ban (white), Dhu, Machree, Lusmore, Rann, Kerne, Boreen, which form no part of the vocabulary of the bards in their best period, but were becoming popular among the nationally minded professional writers of Dublin and the South, eager to give an idiosyncratic Celtic colouring to their verses.

As Flecher was ambitious to reach an audience far beyond the townlands of north Down, he accepted the need to explain his terms, from the vernacular he had known at Moneyreagh, and the Irish he had picked up from books, a complication which would not have suggested itself to the cheerfully unselfconscious Francis Boyle or Robert Huddleston.

Of the books which I have examined only those of Sarah Leech the Donegal peasant girl and Hugh Porter 'the County of Down weaver' are equipped with a similar apparatus, and both of these were sponsored by upper-class patrons with no facility for the vernacular, who considered that the little volumes should be adapted to the linguistic capacity of the audiences which they had assembled from the nobility and the gentry.

When John McKinley brought out a second edition of his verses in Dublin, he left out his vernacular poems, realising that they would not readily be understood, a lack still evident among southern historians of the literature of this island. But we cannot assume a tone of superiority when we recall that, in 1880, a northern amateur philologist was pleased to write, 'Owing to the spread of well managed schools the Scotch accent and the dialect words are passing away.' We may even hazard a regretful guess that perhaps he and his like let slip an Ulster equivalent of *The Merry Muses of Caledonia*.

The linen manufacture in which so many of the bards were engaged and with which the whole rural population was familiar, carried with it a large armoury of technical terms. Many of these belong to the naming of parts still used for the hand-loom and the spinning wheel. But often these were given a vernacular pronunciation, as in *queel* for quill, *wab* for web, and its derivative, *wabster* for weaver, its English equivalent now only surviving in the surname Webster. So, in the preparation of the *lint* (flax) we have *breakin'*, *clovin'*, *heckle*; for spinning, *rock* (distaff), *spit* (axis of wheel), *reel*; and for the spun yarn, measured in *hanks* (four hanks equal one *spangle*), *swift* from which the yarn was wound on *pirns* (bobbins or spools) for the loading of the weaver's shuttle. On the loom the threads were fixed to form the *warp*, with *temples*, as the web progressed, to keep it taut, while the treadles, by foot control, allowed the weft to be built up by the left-to-right-and-back motion of the shuttled thread, the *slays* closing up the threads compactly. Some of the threads clumsily spun might be *twitty* or *crabbit*, difficult to handle smoothly, one against the other. If not used at home, the women took the spun yarn to the weekly linen market in the nearest town. There too weavers sold the complete webs, trimmed and clean of *croppins*, of *stubs*, or *wasted weft*, to the draper or cloth merchant; when spinning was becoming a factory process the yarn would come to the weaver from the spinning mill.

A good account of this may be found in *Domestic Industry in Ireland: the experience of the linen industry*, by W.H. Crawford (Dublin 1972) which is illustrated by contemporary prints and documents, and the poems, 'The Auld Wife's Address to her Spinning Wheel' by Thomas Beggs, 'The Weaver's Triumph' by Edward L. Sloan, and 'The Weaver Question' by Thomas Given.

WEAVER RHYMERS
outside
ANTRIM AND DOWN

Not every working-class writer of verse in the counties of Antrim or Down can be considered one of the Rhyming Weavers; William Shepherd of Larne, for example, whose *Christian Warfare, An epic poem* (1830) runs to about 1,800 lines of heroic couplets, and whose *Temperance and Intemperance* (1832) is 'a dramatic poem in four scenes' of the flattest of blank verse. In additional pieces he writes of his birthplace, Doagh, of Glenarm Castle, of sweet Gleno, and the beauties of Glynn, and in one of the odes in the first volume he refers to 'the Rocky Maidens [which] twinkle with their new bright eyes' when the new lighthouse had been installed on those dangerous rocks. He has somewhere a Standard Habbie poem not in the vernacular, but though he was native of the bards' own ground, he cannot claim to be of their company.

The domestic craft of weaving was in no sense confined to the two eastern counties, and weaving areas elsewhere threw up their poets. Alexander Duffy whose *Poems on Various Subjects* (1817) was printed in Dungannon, is a case in point. Gathering 197 subscribers, fourteen of them clergymen and a number from masters and pupils of the local Royal School, it contains several sets of vernacular Standard Habbie, with references to 'crabbit yarn' and 'wabsters at the treadle' as well as Damon and Chloe, presenting a singular admixture of poetic diction and vernacular grammar.

But an even more absurd figure was Bernard Short (1803–1842) of *Rural and Juvenile Poems* (1821), *The Rude Rhymes* (1824) and two later volumes in 1829 and 1840. In the first he had 330 subscribers, but for the second, inspired more evidently to a superb public relations exercise, he assembled 1,152, including the Lord Lieutenant, the primates of both churches, fifty-eight clergymen of all sorts, forty-two army officers and a clutch of marquesses and lords; his birthplace, Armagh, providing a strong strategic base. In both volumes he stressed his youth, so by internal evidence I have fixed the year of his birth. The date of his death I have assumed from a report in the *Belfast Newsletter* (14 June 1842): 'A man named Bernard Short was drowned yesterday while bathing . . . he was hardly under self-control at the time.' For this would have seemed an appropriate end to a poet who could write:

> Great Alexander, by a callenture,
> Fell feeble, quite exhausted and impure;
> Broke down in spirit and parched up by thirst
> His nose quite sharpened and his eye strings burst.

In the prose preface to the reader, very much in the style later to be associated with Amanda McKittrick Ros, he pleaded, 'Hard and unfeeling would be the heart which would nip with the ungenial frost of invidious criticism, the mental plants of a young and inexperienced bard . . . endeavouring to make the germs of intellect burst through the flinty surface of the world's approbation.'

The Rushlight, a radical Belfast weekly run by Luke Mullen Hope, son of the more famous Jimmy Hope, gave Short's *The Rude Rhymes* and Thomas Stott's *Songs of Deardra* (1825) a joint review which continued for four issues. This concludes by advising the poet to return to 'the Classical avocations of the loom. There are blind cripples and ballad-singers sufficient to fill up the line of business left vacant. – *Finis Mr Short.*'

Another weaver, Robert Donnolly, whose *Poems on Various Subjects, Moral, Religious and Satirical* was printed in Portadown in 1852, has about half a dozen pieces in Standard Habbie in English of a sort. Since he was born in Dublin, we do not expect him to use the central Scots-based vernacular. He does, however, make reference to his craft, as in 'To a Linen Manufacturer':

> With croppins, stubs and wasted weft
> You'll fill a bag with what is left,
> Nor did I think it any theft
> The whole to burn . . .
>
> As for the pay I will not speak,
> I only earned one bob a week
> 'Twould scarcely buy a herring and leek
> For the poor weaver . . .
>
> To curse the flax I think no harm,
> Also the mill that spun the yarn,
> And if I could the warper learn –
> God help him.

This may have some interest to a student of economic history; but, like the rest of Donnolly's verse, it has no other. In his work, as well as in Duffy's and Short's, there is no sense of awareness of a strong metrical tradition and a rich resourceful vernacular, of a friendly competing community of bards sharing a reciprocating even if a declining culture.

The
RHYMING
WEAVERS

As Alexander McKenzie was Gaelus, so too Hugh Porter was Tisander for his contributions to the *Newsletter*, but they were much better known as McKenzie of Dunover, and Porter of Moneyslan, for a poet of the folk was emphatically a poet of a place. So it was Orr of Ballycarry, Campbell of Ballynure, Thomson of Carngranny, Carson of Kilpike, Huddleston of Moneyreagh, Herbison of Dunclug. And each was known and accepted by his neighbours as their spokesman. He derived his material from the life of 'his country'; and the community seemed to require of him the treatment of subjects of general interest, the occasional set of verses rather than the introspective lyric, the local rather than the literary allusion.

From their verses therefore we may learn a great deal about rural society and its structure. The economic basis of it then, the linen manufacture, received voluminous and vigorous attention and comment: from the growing of the lint and the spinning of it, to the weaving on the cottage loom and the selling of the web in the weekly market, flax threaded through the whole fabric of society. So it is convenient to apply to them the title, which they were proud to bear, of 'The Rhyming Weavers', even if weaving was, in some instances, a side-line to smithing or general farming. Most often our bard was a weaver and smallholder, sometimes simply a journeyman weaver without land. One of these last, John Dickey of Rockfield (1818), declared:

> And for my trade, I'm by the by,
>   A lazy-greasy weaver
>
> Upon my loom I'm happier far,
> Than he who rides in mammon's car;
> Wealth never yet has been a bar
>   Tween me and bliss;
> My star's the glorious morning star, –
>   I joy in this.

And again:

> I'll ne'er despise the weaving trade;
> The shuttle's lighter than the spade;
> By it I hae a living made
>   This monie a day;
> There's some high nebs if it should fade
>   Would soon look blae.

Joseph Carson of Kilpike (1831) sets the domestic scene:

> My Bess the house trims up full-tidy,
> An' wi' her wheel sits down beside me,
> While I maun make the shuttles play,
> To crack an' wile the time away . . .

James Orr, though a bachelor, had often seen in a neighbour's house:

His thrifty wife and wise wee lasses span
While warps and queels employed anither bairn.

Carson, though hardly so confident as the bachelor journeyman, Dickey, had come to terms with his condition:

> To haud them weel in brose and claes
> I cheerfu' ply the toiling slays,
> Frae morn till night the shuttle plays,
>   For that's the doom
> Blind fate ordained me a' my days,
>   The damask loom.

With an even sharper sense of his status Porter insisted:

> For manners ye may plainly see
> I learned upon the treadle;
> An' for my state, my stars an' me
> Hae squabbled frae the cradle.

And in 1815 an anonymous versifier appealed to McKenzie to seek a vocation more fitting for a poet:

> Screw up your pipes and gie a tune,
> An' quat the idle filthy loom;
> The talents ye fetched frae aboon
>   Ye bury sair;
> Leave the cursed sticks, an gie a croon
>   An' mount naer mair.
>
> Sic brains as ye hae neer were made
> To hang ay' noddin' o'er a web
> O' auld wives' yarn, whose dirty gab
>   It aften wet,

> To mak' it stick they'd gie't a dab
> An' cough an' spit.

In some districts the weavers made muslin rather than linen, but the economic relationship of the weaver to his employer remained the same. The best known of the century's working-class poets, Francis Davis (1810–1886), learned that trade at Hillsborough, County Down, but ultimately left it to become an urban man of letters as his pen name, 'The Belfastman', implied, so his place is firmly Provincial, and outside our study. Peter Burns (1800–?), of the same county, was also a muslin weaver. In 'An Epistle by way of reproof, To a Muslin Manufacturer', who had recently made a stoppage on the author's work – that is, a fine or deduction from the payment for the work executed – Burns fingers over a wide sequence of varieties and textures, not all of which may be found in the *Oxford English Dictionary*:

> Policates blue, varonas, too,
> Mock dy'd for hawker Nancy;
> Stout changing plaids, with mounting beads,
> And spotting bells for fancy;
> With gauzes light, and plushes bright,
> Mull, stiffen'd book, and veining;
> With shirtings fine, choice window-blinds,
> And corded stripes for staining
> On any day . . .

He continues:

> My parcel sent, by Carman Grant,
> You've settled it by fining . . .

But he will not accept the affront to his craftsman's integrity:

> My rustic muse is craving
> The recent fine, else I'll decline
> The present stroke I'm weaving
>   This very day.

He then recalls the difficulties which he had had to face on this particular job – once again reference is made to 'dressing the threads':

> The drifting snow, not long ago,
> My cabin seem'd to shiver;
> Mid frosty squalls, my crazy walls
> Like aspen leaves did quiver:
> Equal to glass in solid mass,
> My dressing paste was frozen;
> I burned the straw, the 'bove to thaw
> For bedding had been chosen
>   Last new year's day . . .

He concluded, with some pride:

> From henceforth, friend, don't use your pen
> On future slight offences;
> If cloth prove light, return it straight
> And I'll remit expences.

We must, however, remember when each set of verses was written, for, during our period, after the boom years 1799–1806, the weaver's earnings and status declined sharply, to a third of the earlier years' in terms of real wages, most steeply after 1820. So James Orr who died in 1816, could more lightly treat his calling when addressing a fiddler-crony:

> I'm glad, my frien', ye make a shift
> To keep the strings in proper tift;
> Ere this new moon forsake the lift
>   We'll hae some sport
> Tho' my auld treadles sud move swift
>   At midnight for't.

And the convivial James Campbell (1758–1818) could confess:

> I've oft laid down my shuttle
> To meet my friends and bottle,
> And like great Aristotle
>   I have made my brains to reel.

Perhaps the most explicit comment on one of the deepening depressions may be found in Peter Burns' book (1835) nearly twenty years later:

> Then worst of all, the weaving trade
> I had to leave and lift the spade,
> As only half my time I staid
>   Where I was bound;
> The cause of which, work was ill-paid,
>   The nation round.

But for those who were not self-employed, who had to labour the hours ordained by their masters, like Thomas Beggs (1789–1847) who worked at a bleacher's, Sunday seems to have been the only unqualified, guilt-free break:

> At the break of morn I have hastened away –
> On the morn of the Lord, and the poorman's
>   day . . .

Yet even at work, recollection could ease the drudgery, as Campbell remarked, in his song 'Molly Hume':

> Though she was deceiving, for her I am grieving,
> And when I am weaving, I oft times say
> Though my time I wasted, some love I tasted
> When locked within her sweet arms I lay.

Francis Boyle of Gransha has a not dissimilar lyric in his 'Bonny Weaver' (1811):

> When I am weaving on my loom
> I think upon my darlin';
> Tho' she remains in Moira Town
> An' I live in Kilwarlin;
> Resolved in mind for to be kind,
> And never to deceive her;
> Then in return, her love will burn
> For me, her linen-weaver.

The rural economy was so hinged on the whole linen manufacture, the females spinning or preparing the yarn, the men weaving, that even when that schoolmaster from Loughgeel, Hugh McWilliams (1831) went to the nearest large town, Ballymena, he felt impelled to comment in his rough plodding couplets on the yarn and linen markets, familiar sight in every town:

> Behold the yarn market! look what's there
> Of amiable females fine and fair,
> With bunches that their arms can scarcely span
> And others with a few rough dozen run.
> The cautious purchaser withholds a while –
> Cheap! he exclaims – bad stuff, and gives a smile
> The seller now retaliates again,

No better stuff, or yarn was ever spun.
I've fifteen spangle. And I'll beat a crown
There's not a bunch superior in the town.
In six short weeks, the servant maid and I
Spun what you see, 'twould be a sin to lie.
The bargains closed, he pays without delay
She counts it, puts it past, and turns away.

We'll now proceed to where the cloth is sold –
Behold that throng of people young and old,
With webs in readiness – it strikes the hour,
See how they forward rush with all their power
Towards the merchant, whom they well can tell
The quality of what they have to sell;
He views and turns the plies so quick, and then
Bids them a price, and with his ready pen
Claps on a mark immediately, and
Another's waiting, reaching out his hand . . .

There was scarcely a man given to the practice of
verse, if we except schoolmasters, who was not at some
level involved in textile manufacture. Apart from the
weavers, there were many whose trades were also related
to it, reed-makers, for example. John Fullarton was so
employed until 1843, when the introduction of power-
looms 'nearly annihilated it' in his district. Samuel Corry
of Ballyclare, was also a reed-maker. Beggs and James
McKowen were employed at bleach works. Robert
Anderson was a calico-print designer, and others were
not averse to stating their interest, like William Bleakley
of Ballinaskeagh, County Down, by his own report a
super-craftsman of multifarious skills. In his 'Author's
Account' of himself (1840) he declares:

> I could begin and mak' a loom,
> And fit her for the shuttle soon,
> And hing in her a pair o' slays
> That you could handle with some ease;
> And when the same that I would do,
> I could begin and use her too;
> Frae a coarse ten to twice the same
> I could a cloth put frae the chain;
> Mak' temple, shuttles, swifts and wheel
> Or tips as hard as any steel . . .

And Francis Boyle of Gransha, Comber, in his robust narrative, 'The Wife o' Clinkin' Town' drew freely upon the familiar processes:

> I tauld how Sawney payt the wife,
> How limpin' Meg was got wi' bairn,
> How Jock an' Elspa livt in strife,
> An' Sarah sauld ill-counted yarn,
> That Matthew's sowens were thin and sour,
> An' Wattie's Willy skims the kirn
> How Jurkins' daughter turnt a whore
> An' Will the Wabster stow the pirn . . .
> How Jurkins' daughter fought a roun'
> Wi' Mungo's maid an' handlet well
> Till limmer-face aince knocked her down
> Wi' the head-stanart o' her wheel . . .

Again, when he addressed 'a brither bard', John Meharg of Gilnahirk, who is not otherwise known to us, the loom provides the symbol for life's vexations:

> On tw ɑty yarn, wi' eeks sae dry
> Your time does waste, your patience try
> Oure mony knots ye hae to tie

> Cast ower your thumb
> 'Tis time to throw your shuttle by,
> An' quate your loom . . .

When Samuel Thomson, the Carngranny schoolmaster, required a visual equivalent for the hedgehog, it is to the processes of preparation of flax that he instinctively turned:

> Thou looks, Lord save's, arrayed in spikes
> A creeping heckle

for he knew that his audience would take the simile at full value. And when James Orr sums up the communal activities to which tea-drinking is an appropriate, an inevitable adjunct, two of the four are from the same vocabulary:

> At breakin', clovin', kirn an' quiltin'
> 'Tis aye the base that bliss is built on.

It would seem that it is no threadbare metaphor to talk of the warp and weft of that closely wrought society. But, with the years, that fabric disintegrated. Tom Beggs, something of a manic depressive, was positive:

> – since long other days were we smote with this curse
> That if change ever came, it was change for the worse.

David Herbison of Dunclug in his *Midnight Musings* (1848) has a similar dirge in 'The Auld Wife's Lament for Her Teapot':

> The days are past when folk like me
> Could earn their bread,

> My auld wheel now sits silently
> > Aboon the bed.
>
> And well may Erin weep and wail
> The day the wheel began to fail,
> Our tradesmen now can scarce get kail
> > Betimes to eat,
> In shipfuls they are doomed to sail
> > In search of meat.
>
> For that machine that spins the yarn
> Left us unfit our breed to earn.
> O Erin! will ye ne'er turn stern
> > Against your foe,
> When every auld wife can discern
> > Your overthrow.

One may feel the pity of it, while still thinking it late, at that date in the Industrial Revolution, for the expression of such Luddite sympathies. Many of the weaver bards died before the changeover had become fully effective, and the ends of several cannot be traced. McKenzie died a pauper in Belfast in 1839 after peddling religious broadsheets. Beggs succumbed to typhus in 1847. Carson of Kilpike found work in Michael Andrews' factory at Ardoyne. Edward L. Sloan of Conlig, it seems, emigrated. Herbison persisted until 1880, surviving right out of his period like Ossian after the Fenians, and it is in his work that we find the full realisation of the harsh jolting transition. But he was a careful man, became the Ballymena representative of Messrs Finlay Brothers; a Belfast linen firm. James McKowen (1814–1889) lived long enough to receive a pension from his employers.

RURAL
LIFE

THE BOOK CLUBS AND READING

According to the census returns for 1841, Antrim, Down
and Londonderry headed the table of literacy for the
thirty-two counties of Ireland. It is interesting to note
that in the areas which gave us the three principal clus-
ters of rural bards, south Antrim, mid-Antrim and north
and north-east Down, the percentages for literacy were
higher than those for the rest of these counties. This
probably relates to the traditional Scots respect for edu-
cation; but with the uneven distribution of schools much
of this literacy must have been developed at home,
where books were a recognised part of the domestic
equipment. James Orr, for example, was kept at home
because of his delicate health, his father undertaking his
tuition himself. Peter Burns summarised his schooling:

> As I of learning scarce know aught
> Nor never have been grammar taught.

Even for those who attended school the level of
attainment was not impressive. Hugh Porter demon-
strates this:

> First then I naething write by rule,
> For o' the knowledge taught at school,
> Mine was a very scanty share,
> I only learnt the letters there . . .

Edward Sloan of Conlig called himself 'almost uneducated'. Alexander McKenzie 'had not the advantage of a regular education'. John McKinley had only six months' schooling. David Herbison had two years only, the smoke from the turf fire seriously affecting his weak sight.

Usually, however, in adult years the weaver-bard had become a well-read man, more particularly in English and Scots poetry. There is hardly an English poet of repute from Alexander Pope to William Cowper who does not find mention in their books; while Ramsay, Fergusson, Burns and James Hogg were popular, even lesser Scots such as Hector McNeill and Robert Tannahill, the Paisley weaver, had their admirers. For the English, it is likely that anthologies formed the source; although James Thomson's *Seasons* had its Belfast printing, this seems to have had more influence on the academically educated; blank verse and nature-poetry lay outside the canon of the rural poets. I am making no rash guess when I suggest that it was the Reverend Vicesimus Knox's *Elegant Extracts in Poetry Selected for the Improvement of Young Persons* which provided the chief staple. This volume, which came out in many editions, has been the subject of an essay by Edmund Blunden who writes of it 'as in the main a book of eighteenth century taste; for one can find almost everything in it that is likely to be wanted in the ordinary way, besides a number of things that have become difficult to access in other forms of publication'. Hugh Porter in an epistle to his patron, the Reverend Thomas Tighe, asks permission to borrow this very book:

> Among the rest that me attracts
> There's one of which I hear great cracks
> An' that's the *Elegant Extracts*.
>   So if ye hae it,
> Your humble rhymer Sir, expects
>   Or hopes ye'll gi'e it.

> I'll read as much o't as I can,
> An' what I cannot read maun stan;
> I'll keep it clean wi' carefu' han',
>   Nor tear nor burn it,
> An' any time that ye deman'
>   I will return it.

For other anthologies certainly available, I need only refer to the three volumes published by Alexander Mackay and drawn from his journal in the *News-Letter*. These appeared in 1805, 1810 and 1813, and from the last, en-titled *A Collection of Poems on Various Subjects, Volume III*, besides Porter (Tisander), Orr and Robert Anderson, we find Colonial poets like John Stewart, Mary Balfour, the Reverend Willliam Hamilton Drummond, Mrs Aeneas Lamont, Dr William Drennan, Thomas Stott (under his pseudonym, Hafiz) and the ill-fated young man, W.A. Bryson who drowned himself in the Six Mile Water a year later. But we also find a copious selection of Tom Moore's lyrics, Sir Walter Scott's 'Vision of Don Roderick' – twenty-six pages of it (!), Oliver Goldsmith's 'When lovely woman stoops', Dr Beattie's 'Hermit', Bishop Thomas Percy's 'Hermit of Warkworth', selections of James Grahame's *Rural Calendar*, John Scott of Amwell, Peter Pindar, William

Shenstone, William Collins, Thomas Gray, William Cowper (his name misprinted), Robert Southey, Thomas Love Peacock. No Wordsworth as yet, for he was clearly too modern. There are several authors worth mention: Alice Laetitia Aiken, better known as Mrs Barbauld, who had had a Belfast printed edition of her *Poems* in 1774; Mrs Amelia Opie with her 'Orphan Boy's Tale', a poem imitated by at least one of the rural rhymers, and James Montgomery, whose parents had left Gracehill, Ahoghill, a month or two before he was born in Scotland in 1771. Certainly the reading public, whatever its size might have been, was much better versed in contemporary poetry than any here since.

The field of prose-literature lies outside our purview, but it would be fair to say that there was wide acquaintance with Laurence Sterne and Tobias Smollett, and, in a more polemical field, with Thomas Paine and later, with William Cobbett.

Shakespeare seems hardly to have been read. Once, Thomas Beggs saluted James Orr as 'The Shakespeare of the plebian train', but I found no reference to any of the plays. Drama lay some way outside the rural communities' experience, and, anyhow, the Presbyterian code had little place for plays or play-actors. There was a theatre in Belfast where the great players of the day appeared on tour, such as Mrs Siddons in 1802, stouter than she had been thirteen years before. Occasional strolling companies might have been encountered at Larne – where John Templeton saw a production of the then-celebrated *Norval* – at Newry, and even Lisburn or Antrim. James McKowen frequently walked from Lambeg to Belfast to the theatre, but his interest seems to have been unique among the bards.

Colonial poets like Francis Dobbs (1750–1811), of

Lisburn, now and then wrote verse-dramas, but he spent
most of his time in Dublin. Some of them too have left
us rhyming prologues for amateur performances here
and there in the province, and Miss Mary Balfour (1780-
-1819), had her *Kathleen O'Neill*, a grand national melo-
drama in three acts, produced at the Belfast Theatre in
1814. The Reverend Henry Boyd (1756–1832) had his
dramatic pieces printed among his poems in a fat vol-
ume, (Dublin 1793). But drama remained a sophisticated
affair of the town or the book-lined study.

The rural bards' habit of reading was fostered by the
seasonal nature of their manual work. As Robert
Huddleston wrote in an epistle to John Petticrew (1846):

> My denty Jone, while winter r'ugh,
> Wi' frost and sna' keeps back the pl'ugh,
> And barn-men's jabs are few en'ugh
>   The lang storm dreadin';
> While auld guid wife neer tak's the huff
>   Tae see you readin'.

And a highly significant factor was the existence of
country reading societies or book clubs. The members of
these out of their small subscriptions maintained lending
libraries and met regularly for discussion and social
intercourse. In the country towns, as members included
professional men and shopkeepers, the subscriptions
were much higher and newspapers were purchased for
circulation. But for the bards it was the village clubs
which were important.

The names of some of both kinds we know from the
subscription lists in the books of verse, for they were
often generous supporters of the rural poets, even from
some distance. It is no mere chance that the area of the

south Antrim bards was also studded with a little swarm
of clubs – Ballyclare, Doagh first and second, Ballynure,
Carnmoney, Carngranny and the Four Towns: but of
their organisation we know very little. The last men-
tioned, the Four Towns Book Club, drawing its members
from the four townlands of Mallusk, Craigarogan,
Kilgreel and Ballybarnes was the subject of a paper by
the antiquarian, Francis Joseph Bigger in *The Ulster
Journal of Archaeology* (Vol. 8, 1902). This society grew out
of the amalgamations of the Lowtown Club (founded
1790) and the Roughfort Club (founded 1796). The
entrance fee was five shillings and the subscription one
shilling per quarter. On an average forty members
attended and the library consisted of about four hundred
volumes. Of its members at various times several are
known to us in other contexts – Samuel Thomson,
Beggs and Samuel Walker as bards, James Hope for his
political activism and Luke Mullan his brother-in-law.

Of Doagh's two book clubs we have a brief but valu-
able comment from a traveller who passed that way in
July 1808, recorded in the *Belfast Monthly Magazine*
(Vol. 2, p. 423): 'Doagh . . . is a small village consisting of
above thirty dwelling houses . . . It contains nothing
remarkable except its book clubs which are the most
ancient and extensive in this part of the country, the
people generally having a taste for literature. Their club-
room is furnished with globes, maps, etc . . .'

The smaller towns often had clubs, for example,
Banbridge Reading Society was founded in 1795, and
had a monthly subscription of one shilling. A catalogue
of the books held was published in 1838: this contained
1,586 volumes and a large collection of pamphlets. In
its earlier years members numbered 120, in 1837 these
fell to 88, and in 1846 the society ceased to exist. The

subscription, with the declining membership, seems to have been raised to a guinea a year, which proved too high for one rural bard, Joseph Carson, for in his *Poems, Odes, Songs and Satires* (1831), he includes an undated 'Address to the Committee of the Banbridge Reading Society', lamenting his ill-fortune at not being able to afford membership. This was remedied, however, as we learn from another set of verses dated 12 February 1827, in the same volume and entitled 'An Epistle of Thanks to the Committee of the Banbridge Reading Society for their Generous Indulgence to the Author in voting him The Privilege of Using the Books of the Society Gratis'. In this occurs the couplet:

> To thank ye for this precious favour
> Confer'd on me, a rhyming weaver.

In his *Poetical Attempts* (1813), Hugh Porter, that glutton for books, has an address 'To the President and other Members of the Rathfriland Book Society', begging for the loan of Scott's *Lady of the Lake* for a week, and declaring that she would be in excellent company with a preacher (Edward Young of *The Night Thoughts*) and a ploughman (Robert Burns). The person addressed, maintaining the fancy, in response invited Tisander to come and enjoy her in the library, where

> . . . she on lofty shelf reclines
> 'Mongst sages, poets and divines:
> And hither, in their name invites,
> Tisander to the pure delights
> That virtue, wit and solid sense,
> By type and paper can dispense . . .

James Orr in *The Posthumous Works of James Orr,*

of Ballycarry, with a Sketch of his Life (1817) has a poem to a rural reading society, which names among its collection of books, Gibbon, Hume, Johnson's *Lives of the Poets*, and biographies of George Washington and Captain Cooke, and refers to one of its activities, the organisation of formal debate with proper rules of procedure. That the influence of the clubs was felt even beyond its walls we may gauge from John Fullarton's remark that his father's membership of the local reading society brought many useful books to his attention when a boy.

This was all part of a very broad intellectual movement. The Belfast Library or Society for Promoting Knowledge – the Linen Hall Library as it is commonly known – had its origins in the same period, being founded in 1788 with a monthly subscription of one shilling. But this urban institution rapidly outpaced its rural and country town counterparts, based as it was on an expanding and not a declining economy, and not, like them, vulnerable to the hazards of the Famine years and the struggles over land tenure later in the century; it has survived to our own day, an important constituent in the cultural resources of the city, and, it must be remarked, custodian of by far the most comprehensive collections of, among other riches, the little verse-books of the rural bards; though one might doubt if it ever numbered among its members better poets than did the Four Towns Book Club.

Many of these societies were reputed to have been centres of radical thought and sedition, and were believed to have contributed to the militancy of ideas which led to the 1798 Rebellion. Consequently a number are said to have been wrecked and dispersed by the yeomanry. Those that were not, generally seem to have succumbed to the hardships of the forties already mentioned, or to have dragged on and dwindled as the members grew old or died off, and a generation arose which, drilled in the national schools, had their indigenous literary procedures whipped out of them.

The clubs were also places for recreation in story and ballad, as well as the more intellectually strenuous disciplines of debate. Parallel with them, Freemasonry played an important part in the lives of the rural male population. Many of the bards belonged to the craft: Orr, Master of a lodge, McKenzie, Peter Burns, Sloan, Herbison; and, like the reading societies, the lodges figured handsomely in the subscription lists for local volumes of verse. Masonic songs and craft allusions occur in the verses of the poets mentioned. McKenzie even brought out a little book entitled *The Masonic Chaplet* (1832), for which the Ballycarry Lodge 'engaged a certain number of copies to defray the cost of printing'.

So, when we think of the rural bard's integration with his community, it is to be remembered that community itself was altogether more organic and self-contained, not ironed flat by standardisation of education, of the instruments of opinion, not drained by railways and improved roads into, or infected with, a proletarianised urban complex. The hand-loom in the house, the village, the reading room or the Masonic lodge at the crossroads for a brief period offered a unique equilibrium for the emergence of some remarkable talents.

RELIGION

The Scots-settled areas were naturally Presbyterian. It was at Broadisland, where, later, James Orr lived, between Larne and Carrickfergus, that Edward Brice from

Stirlingshire began to exercise his ministry in 1613, and the Presbyterian Church in Ireland took root.

The Episcopal Church of Ireland was the established body which covered the whole island with its dioceses and parishes and levied its tithes upon the inhabitants. So the Presbyterians with all other Dissenters, Baptists, Quakers and later Methodists, were, like the Catholic population, compelled by law to contribute. This was, of course, widely and deeply resented, a sentiment expressed with vehemence by James Campbell:

> The Church and the state have been long linked
> secure,
> We keep the crowd dark and the state keeps them
> poor . . .
> From the fruits of your fields ne'er replenish their
> bowls
> Till ye see how their labour has nourished your
> souls . . .

These lines occur in his 'Adieu to Tithe', written when, judged by the sympathetic Rector of Ballynure to be too poor to pay, the bard was struck-off the tithe roll. As he said, with a fine realism:

> But low, poor and needy, 'tis no shame to me
> The complaint is inherent in my pedigree.

Campbell was the most socially outspoken, the most class-conscious, of the weaver bards. He composed an 'Inscription for the Tombstone of Thomas Paine', author of *The Rights of Man* and so on, which has 171 octosyllabic lines – implying a huge headstone – expounding his views on priest-craft and extolling the virtues of social justice.

Only one minister subscribed to his book. Usually the

clergy, regardless of denomination, seem to have been
called upon and to have given their support. Even Orr,
a fellow-radical, could muster half a dozen. In addition,
many of the books contain respectful elegies for men of
the cloth. The Church of Ireland, particularly in County
Down – and this may have been because the weighty
example of Bishop Percy set the fashion – appear to have
been the most generous patrons, as Reverend Tighe was
to Hugh Porter; although, not unexpectedly, Campbell
has an inscription for the tombstone of a noted rector,
who was 'of gold a real respecter'. But, apart from this,
clergy seem not to have played as significant a part in the
mythology of the rhyming weavers as might have been
expected. A brief epigram by Sam Thomson, who was
politically not radical, may be quoted:

> With formal pomposity, how you can read,
> But meddlers scoffingly mock it;
> For sermons, they say, there's no room in your
>   head,
> So ye bear them about in your pocket:

which indicates that the authority of the preacher gave
no immunity from pointed comment.

There was in the first decades of the century a long
debate within the Presbyterian communion between the
adherents of the New Light or liberal wing, and those of
the Old Light (Auld Licht), the authoritarian conserva-
tives who allowed no flexibility in creed or in interpre-
tation. References to this, in the bards' verses, are usually
on the side of tolerance, though Francis Boyle, in one
instance, robustly takes the Auld Licht side. The best
verses on the controversy, in fact, came from clergymen,
with *The Ulster Synod* (1817) of William Herron of

Ballyclare and *The Thinking Few* (1828) of the Reverend Robert Magill, another County Antrim man. It is a nice coincidence that both were from the territory of the Rhyming Weavers.

The involvement of Dissenting clergy in active politics has been a recurring phenomenon in Ulster. County Down men like the Reverend James Porter of Greyabbey, the satirical pamphleteer, executed outside his own church; the Reverend Dr William Steel Dickson of Portaferry, interned at Fort George; the Reverend Sam Barber of Rathfriland, also imprisoned, were long remembered for their participation in the Rebellion. So it is no surprise that Frank Boyle, that sturdy old Tory, should have commended the Associate Presbytery of Down in these words:

> On proper subjects still you fix,
> The church and state you never mix;
> Nor dip so deep in politics,
>   About the throne,
> As clergymen of other sects
>   That I have known.

> You have been taught in Wisdom's school
> To make the sacred page your rule;
> Not like the keen schismatic fool
>   That does foment
> People to hate and ridicule
>   The government.

Only by teasing the evidence to the edge of plausibility dare I suggest that even a couple of the rural bards had their origins in the pre-Reformation faith. John McKinley in his *Giant's Causeway* (1819) has a set of heroic couplets 'On hearing a discourse delivered by

Wm Neilson, DD, MRIA in the Irish':

> All hail to thee, in whose sweet accents bland
> Flows the primeval language of our land.

This hints at the possibility of the poet having been a native speaker of the old tongue, as he might well have been, coming from the north Antrim coastal area. Had he been, it is likely that he had a Catholic upbringing; but the Reverend William Neilson was a pioneer of Irish studies, though a Presbyterian, running a class in Irish at the Academical Institution (1818–1821) where he was on the staff; and there was at this time an interest in the language and antiquities of the Irish past among educated folk. Certainly, for his second, Dublin, edition (1821) as I have already noted, McKinley whipped up support from the Catholic Maynooth (over sixty names) as well as the Protestant TCD (ninety names). With Joseph Carson, the position is not quite so ambiguous, though doubts may linger. He had an ode to Daniel O'Connell and several other items of an emphatically nationalist nature. While, earlier, O'Connell had corresponded with middle-class Dissenters like John Hancock of Lisburn and Dr William Drennan, I cannot imagine that he had much support from the Protestant working class. But while the clarification of such points may be of sociological interest, we must not give it more attention than it is worth. For it seems that, in that period, only farther west, in County Armagh and the Derry area, were sectarian alignments an important issue, where the challenge of a divided population was evident.

THE TEXTURES OF ACTIVITY

About daily living conditions and the textures of rural activity and circumstance a good deal may be learned or deduced from the vernacular verse. Topics such as the indispensibility of the potato, the remarkable significance of tea in the social pattern, the importance of bacon, the scarcity of meat and fish in the household diet, turf as the basic fuel, whiskey as a beverage and its misuse as a social problem – for weaving seems to have been thirsty work – are subjects upon which much information may be assembled.

And traditional field customs, the churn – the ceremonial cutting of the last standing sheaf of oats – above all, is frequently celebrated. Of seasonable observances the May Eve and Halloween rituals and games are liberally evoked, but Christmas, rather disregarded in the Presbyterian calendar, receives little attention. But then this seems to have been developed later as 'a folk festival' by Charles Dickens and the Prince Consort, so we have no Christmas trees, no carols, no waits, no Christmas presents. Rush crosses were apparently confined to the native Irish areas, and the Easter dyed eggs and their 'trundling' concentrated on the slopes of Cavehill, so eloquently described by Lieutenant William Reed in his *Hill of Caves* (1818). Peasant beliefs in good and bad luck, in witches capable of changing their physical form, go far to possess the supernatural world utterly.

Like Ulster country folk generally, the Rhyming Weavers showed little appreciation of scenery or natural detail beyond a limited range of wild flowers and the calls of a few birds; the corncrake being most often reported. For descriptions of nature we should need to turn to several of the Colonial poets such as James Stuart or William Carr who worked in the contemporary literary tradition of the 'Prospect Poem'. For detailed observation of John Clare's kind we look in vain. In fact, the Northamptonshire peasant is unique among countrymen poets in these islands.

THE SINGING CLASS

In that essay by Samuel Ferguson, published in 1836, to which I have referred, there is an interesting account of another rural activity among young folk in mid-Antrim:

> Before leaving the district we would however mention a custom peculiarly characteristic of these descendants of the countrymen of Burns. In some parts of the country, in the wild district of Glenwhirry, in particular, they have stated meetings at one another's houses and on a certain evening, commencing with instructions in sacred music given by a teacher hired or elected for the purpose. After the completion of this lesson, the meeting resolves itself into what may be called a school of versification. And each person present is called on in turn for an original couplet. The verses produced on such an occasion, are as may well be supposed, neither very poetical in spirit nor elegant in diction; but a collection of them would be found to embody a good deal of rough humour.

This, firmly based on Ferguson's boyhood recollections of Glenwhirry where, for some time, he lived, has its confirmation in Alexander McDowell's 'Sketch of the

Author's Life' which prefaced *The Posthumous Works of James Orr* (1817), in which 'It is said that his earliest essays in poetry were exhibited in attending singing-schools, where the young people of the country acquire the very imperfect knowledge of sacred music they possess. It is usual upon these occasions, to sing lines of bad poetry to worse music; and these are often the spontaneous effusions of the moment. In this kind of doggerel verse, Orr first commenced his poetical career, and it is said, far excelled his competitors.'

Until the controversial introduction of instrumental music much later in the century, only unaccompanied hymn or psalm singing was permissible in the meeting-houses. So these 'singings' were, in effect, something like choir practices; but since there was a Calvinistic taboo on the use of the 'sacred' words in utilitarian practising, neutral or emphatically secular words were fabricated to fit the tunes: out of this must have developed the singing-games and making of rhymes both Ferguson and McDowell describe.

In the account David Herbison gives in the preface of his *The Snow Wreath* (1869), and repeats word for word in his 1879 volume, *Children of the Year*, there is no reference to 'sacred music'. 'In those days the young people of the neighbourhood were accustomed to meet for amusement at rural "singings", where any person who could manage to manufacture an extempore verse was at liberty to repeat the lines, whilst the members of the company were bound to sing them. My first attempt at rhyme was at one of these little gatherings in a neighbouring barn. I did not like either the character or composition of the verses introduced; and, on the impulse of the moment, I determined to try my hand at one better suited to the presence and hearing of many simple but

pure-minded country girls in the assemblage. I succeed-
ed to the manifest admiration of all present.'

The only exact reference among the verses of the
bards to this, is in John Dickey's 'Country Singin'',
which, in fifteen *The Holy Fair* stanzas, musters the lads
and lasses 'To yon wee house beside the hill', to practise
'The certain set o' tunes', 'For order and for beauty's
sake/ Each sex in different classes'. But most of his
description in the verse and in his prose notes, is con-
cerned with the singing games which follow – 'False
Priest and True', 'The Widower from the War Returned',
'The Frisky Dance' – with the formations and gestures
these involve.

Whether being located in a barn and not the house of
one of the company determined the utterly secular
nature of the occasion, or whether 'singings' of both
kinds took place cannot easily be decided, for we do not
know enough about them; but it is clear that the singing
of secular songs was highly popular in the rural commu-
nity. Many of the more lyrical sets of verses in the rural
bards' volumes have the names of tunes or airs attached
to the titles. Mostly these seem to be of Scottish origin
like 'The Flowers o' the Forest', or 'Lochaber' or from the
common treasury to which Robert Burns' name is
affixed. Now and then we may note a title like 'General
Munro' which refers to the Rebellion, or, in James Orr's
first volume, 'Savourna Deilish', which looks like an
attempt at phonetic spelling. However, the ready manner
in which tunes were taken up, carried here and there,
altered, makes this an area of glorious uncertainty. In
Robert Burns' 'Strictures on Scottish Songs and Ballads'
in the fifth volume of James Hogg's and William
Motherwell's edition of his works (1852), we read of
'Jockie's Gray Breeks': 'Though this has certainly every

evidence of being a Scottish air, yet there is a well-known tune and song in the North of Ireland called, "The Weaver and his Shuttle", which, though sung very much quicker, is every note the very tune': and in another note 'To a Rose Bud', Burns remarks 'This is the composition of a — Johnston, a joiner in the neighbourhood of Belfast. The tune is by Oswald, altered, evidently, from Jockie's Gray Breeks'. So notions of originality or of plagiarism are irrelevant quibbles. The moral of Brecht's *Caucasian Chalk Circle* is that that belongs to him who makes the best use of it.

Certainly it would seem from the localised love songs set to well-known tunes, from the songs of conviviality, the Masonic songs, which occur in their books, that one of the rural bard's social functions was to fit expected or required words to acceptable airs so that the stuff of local song was continually renewed.

No
FEMALE BARDS

There do not appear to have been any women makers of vernacular verses or, what would have been more likely, makers of songs, among the weaving communities, like the Scots Tibbie Pagan of the whisky-bothie, or Jean Glover the travelling woman, whose 'Ca' the yowes' and 'O'er the Moor' became as well-known as 'Auld Robin Gray' and 'The Land o' the Leal' of Lady Barnard and Lady Nairne, in their native land.

Books of verse by such poets as Mary Balfour of Limavady, Hannah Morison of Newry, Mrs Aeneas Lamont and her two daughters, Anne Elliott of Armagh and others, came from the printers, in some number, but these had an upper-class, a middle-class or an urban origin, and their authors fall into the Colonial or Provincial categories. None of these made use of the vernacular, although it is surprising that the Belfast-born Mrs Elizabeth Hamilton (1758–1816) has her own place in Scottish literature with 'My Ain Fireside'.

From County Donegal there was 'the blind poetess' Frances Brown (1816–1879) who had a vogue across the water for some years, graduating from the *Irish Penny Journal* to the *Athenaeum*, and having her books published in London and Edinburgh. But from the same county, the Dublin-printed *Poems on Various Subjects* (1828) by Sarah Leech, with an engraved portrait of the young peasant at her spinning wheel, should have relevance to our theme. Living in the Scots-planted part of the county, daughter of a linen-weaver, schooled for only six months, she shares much of the lifestyle of our own bards farther east. So it is not unexpected when she uses the vernacular in Standard Habbie and *The Cherry and the Slae* stanzas, and she accepts the role of the spinner:

> Wi' heck weel-teeth'd and spit renewed
> I sat me down to spin contented.

She can offer a glimpse of folklore:

> And elf-shot stanes your kye ne'er blight
> By wounds unseen.

A vehement supporter of the Protestant, Anti-Repeal cause, she addressed the Brunswick Club, to whose President and officers the volume was dedicated:

> Petition Wellington and Peel,
> To guard the bulwarks of the nation
> And show their wish for Ireland's weal
> By crushing Dan's association.

An example of her light-vernacular at its best may be gauged from a single stanza:

> Ilk lass maun ha'e a snaw-white goun
> Wi' span-lang flounces wavin' roun',
> Some weel-plait straw upon her croun,
>   And ribbons gay,
> While hose weel starched an' right-left shoon
>   Her feet display.

That allusion to her 'right-left' shoes makes an interesting point in the development of footwear design, the change over from interchangeable shoes to those made for right and left feet specially. This can be related expressly to another stanza, this time by Samuel Thomson from faraway Lylehill, from his 'Elegy to My Auld Shoen' in *Poems on Different Subjects, partly in the Scottish Dialect* (1793):

> I'l say't, great pains I took, alway,
> To gie ye baith alike fair play;
> I chang'd ye duly ilka day
> I pat ye on.
> But now, gude faith, I'm e'er right wae,
> To see ye done.

For the Carngranny schoolmaster obviously had shoes of the older non-particular kind.

But most of Sarah Leech's other verses are in standard English, and deal with sentimental or religious themes; 'The Parting Lovers', 'The Village Maid', 'Prepare to meet Thy God . . .' She is rather a dull than a downright bad rhymer. Like her contemporary whose book, *The Poetical Works of Janet Little the Scotch Milkmaid*, was published in Ayr in 1792, she belongs to the host of humble versifiers so eagerly taken up by fashionable patrons, which happened to few of the bards.

THE RURAL BARDS
of
COUNTY DOWN

Although the Dromore power-house of patronage was at work from its County Down base for the first decade of the century, it had less effect than might have been expected upon the fortunes of the weaver poets than upon their edcuated counterparts of the Colonial kind. Only one countryman from the neighbouring fields, William Cunningham (1781–1804) of Magherabeg, a sad and short-lived schoolmaster who had the good or ill-fortune to look like Oliver Goldsmith, was taken into the Bishop's circle. He wrote only a few rather dim verses. The group's chief triumph was the impressive launching of Thomas Romney Robinson's *Juvenile Poems* (1806), and a charming addendum to this may be read in Hugh Porter's lines 'On seeing his name in Robinson's Book', with 'Esquire' appended to it, among the subscribers, an unusual distinction for 'a County of Down Weaver'.

> O Robinson! may laurel green
> Ay blooming on thy brow be seen,
> And may nae crabbed critic, keen

> Thy fame besmear;
> But for thy bays, I ne'er had been
> Created Squire.

Alexander McKenzie's remarkably successful volume came out in 1810, before Bishop Percy's death. Porter's, three years later, carries an editorial tribute: 'he fanned into fame the humblest attempt of the weakest muse and encouraged the efforts of the deserving in every line', and among the verses there is an elegy to the memory of the late Lord Bishop:

> Attend ye worthies – do, ah! do
> Produce the funeral song;
> I'll chant my little requiem too –
> But far behind the throng:

No others of the rural bards seem to have received the episcopal commendation. The poets of County Down were rather separate persons with little or none of the class companionship of the book clubs, or share in the recognition which envelops the County Antrim poets who maintained a network of friendship and correspondence with each other. Francis Boyle (*c*.1730–?), the oldest of these, in his *Miscellaneous Poems* (1811) does refer to two bards of Gilnahirk, and he has in his volume a complimentary address to one of them, John Meharg, but that is all we know of the latter.

Boyle, apparently a generation older than Robert Burns, used Standard Habbie to good effect. Of 'Fairy Thorn' he writes:

> 'Tis lang sin' that auld thorn was plantit,
> An' auld wives say it lang was hauntit,
> Wha fairy tribes there danc't an' rantit,

> Upo' the green,
> An' music of the wan'erers chantit,
> On Halloween.

And his cuckoo comes in no borrowed plumage:

> An' after a' thy rhyming din
> Just like the lave o' thy fause kin
> Thou lea'st a scabby get behin'
> To whinge an' greet
> Without a feather on its skin
> To turn the weet.

His Auld Gelding is no imported beast; it belongs among the drumlins:

> Thy bonny face we' star an' snip,
> Thy sleekit hide, thy weel-turn't hip.
> Thy tail or mane, I winnae clip
> Or poll thee bare;
> Like them that gang on board a ship
> For Glasgow Fair.

> When snaws lie lang an' frost is keen,
> An' neither grass nor foliage seen
> I gather whins that's young an' green
> An' them prepare,
> An' feed thee with them morn an' een
> To sleek thy hair.

His trade as blacksmith was a source of pride, thoroughly understood and appreciated, as he handed over a new made plough to a clergyman-customer:

> Dear Revern't Sir, here is your plough;
> Her timber's seasont well enough,

Cut frae the bank above the sheugh
    Where guid ash grows;
He puts nae rubbish, dos'd or rough,
    In clergy ploughs.

If ye hae got a guid ploughman,
A fittie-fur an' fittie-lan',
That never jostle, snap or stan',
    An' driver guid,
Than ilka day in sax hours gaun,
    She'll turn three rood.

This pleugh's no' made to rin on wheels,
Like them at Hampton town or Sheals,
Or others, made by Scottish chiels,
    Poor silly gowks:
Sic pleughs wad never till our fields
    Among the rocks.

There's ither pleughs are cried up neist,
Wi' a pot metal sock an' reest,
Sald for five guineas at the least,
    Enormous price!
They'll no' be bought by any priest,
    They're a' owre wise.

He watched the thatcher with a craftsman's eye:

The guid saugh scobes that were well bent,
He drove their points a' up aslant;
This hindert rain to get a vent,
    That through might seep.

And when the young upstarts at the trade demanded

the extortionate wages of two shillings a day plus their morning tea, he decided that henceforth:

> We'll theek wi' slate

But, as this with the other crafts was worked into the texture of the community's life and death, when Ned Mills was dead, the master-thatcher:

> His auld grey head lies at the wa',
> His house weel-theekit wi' a scraw
> He cares na how the tempest blaw.

Master himself of all practicalities, he naturally could compute the cost of a wake for the dead and the traditionally necessary refreshments:

> Gae buy a p'und o' Indian weed,
> An' pipes to smoke when I am dead,
> An' whisky bought frae Matthew Read
> > O' his distillin',
> There's a' the money that ye need
> > That's fifty shillin'.

And, if, with the free-handed custom of the vernacular bard, he took a line from Allan Ramsay's page, he bettered it with one of his own and presented a valid image:

> She turn'd the brunt side o' her shin
> Wi' pictures on't o' a' her kin.

Boyle provides an excellent example of the integrated bard: with freshness and honesty he expresses the values and ideals of his own folk, staunchly Auld Licht in the theological debate, and says so: describes the disasters which followed on the heels of Rebellion as he knew it:

On Pike Sunday, near to Moneyrea.

He understands and assesses the gamut of skills that the country life requires, has a kindly but keen eye for beast and bird, knows the time and place for the love lyric to the sonsy lass, and the sharp satire on the cheating grocer. He could make when needed, the bawdy jest; Hiberno-Scot certainly, but with the same tradition behind him as Robert Burns had. I feel that he belongs like him to a broader patrimony, with Chaucer and Breughel, with Rowlandson and Cobbett, a tiny figure in that company, but firm and wholesome as a hazelnut.

Compared with Boyle, both Porter and McKenzie are obviously thinner stuff: the latter hardly at all flecked with the rich idiosyncratic language of the Scot, sentimental, pseudo-literary; the former, self-concerned, patron-orientated. Only once in 'The Muse Dismissed', does Porter come near to rendering the pulse and effort of labour. But then, McKenzie was Gaelus and Porter Tisander in their public roles. Boyle's rough hands would have rejected such specious elegance. He was no Meliboeus, never once thought of himself as having a muse. In his 'Farewell to Granshaw', he declares 'my age is now eighty', and a reader will readily feel that Boyle's sturdy verses are seasoned by a life's experience, and, like his plough, were made to last a long time and many weathers.

Peter Burns of Kilwarlin was born in 1800, went to a Church of Ireland Sabbath School, and was lent books by a Presbyterian clergyman. As his book, *Poems on Various Subjects* (1835), was dedicated to a seceding minister of Saintfield, that was probably his sect. Married at nineteen, he began versing at twenty-eight. Much of his rhyming has, as we will have noted, to do with his trade of muslin-weaving. He too was a Freemason. In so much he is typical. Only, in one set of verses, addressed 'To a Murmuring Stream' (distilled and purified by the sun), does he cast a sidelong glance at any other craft or process:

> The operator, to thy still
> No kieve or boiler doth require
> No metal tubes, by founder's skill
> Made proof against external fire;
> No frame of brick whereon to rest
> A flavour fine thus to procure –
> No tits or cocks by any pest
> Are there cast by, as if impure . . .
> No excise-quack, thy depth shall sound;
> Content you daily glide along;
> You're duty-free, to no man bound –
> To every sect thou dost belong.

We may well wonder where he picked up the finer points in poteen-making, but in word and wit there is a lightness of touch in this, far outside the scope of William Bleakley of Ballinaskeagh, *Moral and Religious Poems* (1840), whose language, though sometimes Scots, is always flat and prosaic, recording the skills appropriate to his 'peculiarly mechanical turn of mind', as he himself describes it. I have mentioned his success at loom-making and its ancillary trades; to this we must add cart-building, furniture-making:

> Down frae the stead for her an' Jimmy,
> Een to the cradle for young Sammy.

He could 'case' you a clock, mend your shoes, if necessary, sink your well, and, though confessedly ignorant of music:

> Mak' a fiddle that
> Would speak distinct the sharp an' flat
> Wi' pleasing treble, counter, base,
> To screed you off the Chevy Chase.

But he had no skill whatsoever to communicate the tactile qualities or the human significance of the mountain of objects which he must have constructed in that busy workshop.

His contemporary, William Anderson, of Saintfield, now of Lurgan, who published his *Original Poems* (1841), is a bore of another kind. As a schoolmaster, in this, his second book, his eye is above his calling and its minutiae. He celebrates the famous night of the Big Wind, 6 January 1839, the providential escape of our beloved Queen and her Royal Consort from assassination, and the utility of steam, by means of which he could travel from Lisburn to Belfast in twelve minutes. He comments on the crowds of Irish labourers passing through Lurgan on their way to Scotland and England in search of work, and provides a brief description of Waringstown. The rest of his 246 pages are taken up with sacred, moral and elegiac pieces, if, of any interest at all, of interest to the social not the literary historian, since as an educated man he eschewed the vernacular, the language of feeling.

With Lurgan-born Joseph Carson of Kilpike, *Poems, Odes, Songs and Satires* (1831), we are back among lively words, personal, emotional. Though several of the County Antrim weavers were strongly political, Carson, unlike them, was always eager to name his enemies; one

troubled him intensely, 'Our country's shame, vile
Castlereagh'. He held a poor opinion of King George IV
and his way with women. He aimed a late broadside at
the much lampooned Thomas Stott. More than Porter,
but in a smaller, more subjective way than Boyle, he par-
ticipated in the life of his community. For example, he
shared a newspaper with others:

> You sit looking over the News at your ease,
> And just send the paper whenever you please,
> With orders imperious to handle it clean
> To read it in haste and return it again
> As if we were outcasts of blind Fortunatus.
> And you, like good fellows, were sending it gratia.

A ready rhymer, apt to slip into a jingle, nevertheless
he displays a wide prosodic variety and handles Standard
Habbie with confidence, and his lines are usually
weighted with sense of some sort; critical support for
Daniel O'Connell, abuse of Bernard Short's bad rhymes,
approval for Jack Lawless, the well-known nationalist
journalist. It is perhaps from the large number of refer-
ences to Irish people that one somehow accepts the idea
that Carson was a Catholic. Even a couplet such as

> Father Keating's famous pages
> That paint the deeds of former ages . . .

tends to support this, for it is unlikely that a rhyming
weaver of Scots origin and firmly rooted in their culture,
would ever have heard of that old Irish historian. And
when, elsewhere, abruptly he remarks:

> a man I heard abuse my creed,

his particular ancestry seems beyond doubt.

His democratic views are beyond doubt. He urges the electors of Preston to return Cobbett to Westminster. He attacks authority in Church and State:

> With rents and tithes they heap on taxes,
> To keep us poor, to crush and vex us,
> To deck the minions of the court,
> And keep up jilts for George's sport,
> To pay police to keep us humble
> And blow our brains out if we grumble.

Yet, with all his fervent opinions on affairs of state, he could find time to lilt a typical lyric of his tribe:

> Among the braes the burnie strays
> Wi' gentle tinkling sound,
> The vi'let blue and primrose too
> Adorn the dells around;
> The heart that warms to nature's charms,
> When vernal breezes blaw,
> Will find the rose or virgin snows
> Compris'd in Sally Law.

I have remarked earlier that among the country folk of that and later periods there seems to have been little appreciation of the picturesque in their experience. This was, of course, a sensitivity or an awareness which had only been defined in the previous century among the English cognoscenti; it had not rippled out through society. So it is interesting to find Carson alone among the rural poets commenting on the subject, this in 'An Epistle to Mr James Hogg', which begins with the unusually objective:

> Accept a minor poet's lays
> Frae Erin's shore.

Launched on his theme he continues:

> Yet a' these rural beauties lie
> Unnoticed by a bardie's aye',
> Unsung in heart felt melody
>   's enchanting sound,
> While every Scottish mountain high
>   Is classic ground
>
> 'Tis no' but we hae bards enou',
> That patriotic are an' true,
> Our hamely rural scenes they view,
>   Wi' heart felt pleasure
> But hae no' sung, except a few,
>   In rustic measure . . .
>
> But ne'er a ane among them deigns
> To sing in sweet an' hamely strains
> The beauties o' the rural plains,
>   And cottage joys,
> Where harmless mirth an' pleasure reigns,
>   An' care destroys.

The ambiguity of that last line, poised between the opposites – mirth destroys care, or care destroys mirth, hints at a fundamental unease in the poet's estimate of the rural condition. Scenery is all right, but in the midst of it, we have hungry days . . . It would be relevant to point out that landscape painting was slow to start in the north of Ireland, and only with Andrew Nicholl (1804–1886) was a resident artist beginning to concern himself with that alone, and becoming able to live by it.

It is only when Carson turns back to his community for his material that he writes with full confidence; as when in excoriating a bogus pill-manufacturer, he suggests that a tailor's job would fit him better:

> As you're so dapper, neat and nimble,
> Tak' up the lap-board, goose and thimble,
> An' seated on the tailors' boss,
> Your limber-bearers lapp'd across,
> You may be taught without delay,
> To 'stitch the louse' and 'jag the flea'.

Another example of commerical dishonesty comes under his lash, in 'My Auld Mither's Address to Mr Hugh B—e, Agent for the East Indian Tea Company':

> Confound your Indian trash, B—e,
> 'T'as neither taste or smell of tea . . .
> May heaven preserve the auld Chinese
> An' may no bitter ruffian breeze
> To blast their infant budding trees,
>   E'en intervene –
> They send us o'er the best o' Teas
>   Baith black an' green.
>
> Sweet beverage, mix'd wi' yellow cream,
> My morning draught at night the same
> My wakenin' thought – my sleeping dream
>   Were't no' for thee,
> Langsyne this poor auld wrinkled frame
>   Had ceased to be.

Yet in all this celebration and condemnation of the multifarious circumstances of a life vividly experienced and fluently expressed, as with most of his kind, Carson faced and railed against the ultimate economic limitations of his class:

> O Poverty! the chiefest bane,
> Inflicted on the rhyming train,
> By thee how stinted is my store,
> Of knowledge of the days of yore;
> Full sore (untaught in school or college)
> I feel the want of useful knowledge.

Writing over twenty years later, Edward L. Sloan of *The Bard's Offering: A Collection of Miscellaneous Poems* (1854) displays something of the same democratic spirit, but with a diminished use of vernacular, never trying his hand at any of the characteristic Scots stanzas. A weaver and a Freemason, the dedication of his book to William Sharman Crawford, leader in Parliament of the northern farmers' struggle to legalise Tenant Right, makes his allegiance clear. Aware of technical progress, he saluted 'this new age of science and of wonders':

> When steam's superior praise is loudly hurled,
> And telegraphs electric span the world.

In this and in much else, he makes us aware that, by mid-century, the rural fabric was disintegrating. Stylistically he is moving into the Provincial category. Much of his verse is cast in the common measure of the hymn-book and has lost the flavour of daily speech. There is a hint, physically, of the break. His 'Adieu to the Green Fields of Erin', a farewell to the master and members of his Masonic lodge, suggests that he is contemplating emigration to America.

A piece which has no parallel in the weavers' literature, 'The Fast – A Dialogue' is couched in flat clumsy blank verse – a form of verse they practised rarely and showed no skill with – but its interest is considerable.

Briefly, Mr E who is not going to church, preferring to enjoy the open air, on the occasion of 'a fast day' for the success of the Queen's armies in 'the approaching strife' (possibly the Crimean War) encounters Mr B who challenges him. Mr E responds with a pathetic tale of an evicted unemployed man, who, with his little family, is enduring the real fast of starvation. When Mr B declares that it is the nature of the economic system which necessitates such a circumstance, Mr E bursts out, and the verse takes on a vigour:

> Then I would say, reform; reform at home;
> Reform around – each in his private sphere –
> All in their public character; talk less
> About reform, and do; drag forth the slaves
> Who wander in our midst, to public gaze,
> Give to the poor man work and wages for't,
> Nor, while we work him, starve him to the death;
> Care for him more than we would for a beast –
> House him and clothe him, give him mental food
> And educate his young, but let him work
> For all, he will not shun the given task –

Words which in Conlig in 1854 must have sounded like the recently published Communist Manifesto, if anyone in those parts had heard of it.

Sloan's sympathy with his class is most evident in 'The Weaver's Triumph', in which a weaver cheated by 'a draper' turns the tables. But the longest piece which stands as a useful record is 'The Year's Holidays'. This, in octosyllabic couplets, itemises the folk-customs and superstitions which, in a prose-note by the author, are described as 'firmly believed in the bulk of the population . . . in that part of the County Down to which I belong'. The New Year wisps of straw flung through the door, Pancake Eve, the dyed eggs of Easter, the yarrow under the pillow, are threaded through with the sports and games of the young, culminating in the Christmas festivities, for by this date Prince Albert and Dickens had made them popular.

Another poet who wrote of the country superstitions and magical practices was the schoolmaster, John Williamson (1791–1839), who came from Armagh to open a classical academy in Ardglass, where young men could be trained for the professions. His volume, *Poems on Various Subjects* (1839), called upon five hundred subscribers, of whom Joseph Carson seems to have been one. In this, the pedagogue offers the virtues of emigration:

The Texas are now a comparative waste,
And so large that they may not be peopled in haste
And the natives reside on the rivers and shore
By the profits of Commerce increasing their store –

He sings the praises of 'the complicated vapour-mov'd machine' and 'the amazing force omnipotent of steam'. He marvels at the velocity of light, which 'would in one second pass full eight times round the world'. He names the colours of the spectrum in a handy mnemonic:

Red, orange, yellow, green, blue, indigo,
And violet, succeeding in a row.

He has read and imitates Byron in anapaestic ballads and romantic tales of 'The Parricide, or the Haunted Inn of Wolfswald'. He casts a sympathetic glance on the 'Pleasures of the Sabbath', in Spenserian stanzas, on the 'week-worn' labourer resting in his rude bed, the 'sallowfaced' artisan out for a walk, the child 'that scarce exceeds an infant's years' released from a seventy-two hour week, and the bankrupt immured indoors who can only come out without fear of arrest, on Sunday. Obviously a Provincial and not a Vernacular writer, only his 'May Eve' lodges him properly in the rural context. The traditional tricks are here; the snail under the wooden bucket, and the rest. He makes more of the witch, before daybreak, gathering the early dew in her cloak with the old cry of 'Come a' to me' to the beggaring of her neighbours, and of the farmer who, overhearing her, adds 'And half to me!':

> His vessels all were overflown
> With milk that season, not his own ...

His school was clearly not one of those even briefly attended by the weavers' children. County Down had several of these academies, the best known being that at Rademon which the Neilsons or Nelsons – they used both forms of the name – carried on for several generations, turning out future Catholic bishops and Presbyterian moderators. The Reverend William Neilson, the Irish scholar heard preaching by John McKinley, and the Reverend Isaac Nelson, then head of the school, were among Williamson's subscribers.

When Carson was working in a Belfast factory in the sixties, we find him contributing verse to the *Ulster Magazine*. Another County Down contributor was Robert Huddleston of Moneyreagh. His two volumes of verse are dated 1844 and 1846, and with these we are closer to the poetical territory of Frank Boyle, though Huddleston makes no reference to the older poet. Of Ulster writers of the immediate past, it is Samuel Thomson, the Lylehill schoolmaster, whose work he knew most thoroughly. But, with Boyle, he has a marked cultural affinity, in the intensity of his identification with the folk, in the range of his prosodic devices, and his love for the local speech. Yet, by 1846, this was appearing as a conservative trait. In the 'Prefatory Remarks' to the collection of that year, he writes: 'It has been said that I denounce the language of the day, and am an unfashionable creature ... But being a rustic born and bred where the language in its aboriginal idiom is spoken, it has a peculiar charm to me above all other modes of speech. What then remains for me, but to follow the language which nature has given me?'

The lengthy prose prefaces to both books provide a unique manifesto on the aims and practice of the rural bard. Original ideas jostle with an exuberant rhetoric, but the writer's sincerity and his stout democratic attitude are never in doubt. And the story of how the idea of rhyming first came to him, 'scouring a dyke sheugh', has an authentic ring. Here, if ever, speaks an autochthonous bard.

In May 1868, as he records in his unpublished journal, Hugh Leslie Stewart, a young Belfast literary dabbler, went with Francis Davis and Henry McDonald Flecher, who had been a schoolmaster there, to visit Huddleston at Moneyreagh. 'Our host met us at Ballygowan station with a *rale owl shanrydan* – a covered cart without a top – musical for want of oil and preserved from ruin and the cleaving influence of the sun by the clabber which its wheels had mercifully bedaubed it. "That's the wy A pents my carriage. A jist let the new wash aff the owl," said the country bard as he bade us get in, and mounted the dickey himself to steer us to his home. I could not give a much better description of our host than to say he was very like his own carriage.' Stewart's opinion that in Huddleston's verses 'One often meets with something that threatens an idea, and not infrequently with a sterling idea chastely and well expressed, but somehow or other these last seem accidental . . . They are, as Flecher says, "diamonds in a dung-hill"', no more than demonstrates the gulf between the Vernacular and the Provincial.

In his first book, the narrative poem, 'Doddery Willowaim', is somewhat in the vein of 'Tam o' Shanter', with a liberal use of assonance in place of full rhyme, carried with considerable gusto; it is crammed with banshees, the Devil, imps of Hell and witches frolicking through a night of great storm. 'The Lammas Fair' in the 'Christ's Kirk' stanza is a lengthy and expansive evocation of the fair in Belfast, at Lang Brig En, with all the raucous turmoil of such occasions. With this, his tribute to Samuel Thomson's work, a couple of items in Standard Habbie – one of them on medicinal salts – and a handful of lyrics of the weavers' kind, show his range the-matically and linguistically. The second volume, as counterweight to Doddery, has 'Tom Tearaway', in heroic couplets of a Scots-homespun texture, which tells another tale of the folk, of the subterfuges and fate of a thieving neighbour. In this there are one or two touches of pleasing natural description, never a strong suit with the rural poets:

> The bracken rustled o'er the neighbouring brae,
> The clustering crawtree blossomed round the slae . . .

Huddleston turned out lyrics, many of them: 'The Lovely Lass o' Creevy Ha' ', 'The Bonnie Lass o'

Tullquilly', 'The Bloomin' Sweet Lassie O'Broadly Brae', 'The Sweet Bloomin' Lassie o' Lovely Drumreagh', 'Pretty Jane Hamill, The Lass of the Falls', which display a wide if monotonous bouquet of affections. Of his song 'Nannie', he notes 'Burns sang of a Nannie as well as many thousands before him; But you will find by inspection his Nannie and mine to be quite different,' for he had a true comprehension of the function of the folk-bard in the folk-culture within which he existed.

What Stewart could not appreciate was that his encounter with Huddleston was that of two distinct cultures, the Victorian urban colliding ignorantly with the rural traditional, that the, to him, illiterate jingler was in reality one of the last of the folk-bards, custodian of a richer, more closely-wrought heritage than his, free of a language and a prosody which drew upon three centuries of a nation's literature, not from the daily newspaper and the current popular novels of the lending library.

One of the visitors to Moneyreagh on that day in May 1868, and a far older friend of Huddleston's than either Davis or Stewart, Flecher had an unusual career for a country schoolmaster. The contrast with the earlier pathetic Hugh Tynan of Donaghadee (1782–1802) could hardly be sharper. Tynan brought out his poems in 1800, and had a posthumous volume issued in 1803 to raise funds for his impoverished and aged mother. He worked two hours a day in the local Customs House and taught school the rest of the time. The Reverend Samuel Burdy, alone of the Dromore circle, was among his four hundred subscribers, together with those two charitable friends, James Orr and Samuel Thomson.

Tynan's verse is clothed with eighteenth-century poetic diction: feathered choir; drowsy swain; mighty

fluid element (the sea), and snow-white fluid element
rich (milk), are fair examples. He inveighed against 'the
modern blasphemies' of Thomas Paine, later to be
Huddleston's intellectual hero; he recorded the view
from his office door:

> E'en now the breeze with gentleness wafts o'er
> The packet from the neighb'ring Scottish shore . . .
> Here we may view the plodding sons of care,
> With cautious fear import their Scottish ware;
> Lest keen excise-men, with a watchful eye,
> Unhappily their smuggled goods espy . . .

Although this must have been a challenge to his part-
time profession, it was cock-fighting, bull- and badger-
baiting, which roused his deepest indignation. But his
words are so stale and shop-soiled that we turn from this
ineffectual, if angry, little shade with some relief.

Flecher was born at Ballinderry, County Antrim, in
1827. He taught school in Moneyreagh, County Down,
until about 1866. Thereafter he became a mill manager
in Belfast for a short period, before emigrating to Texas
in 1871, where he was still living in 1909. His verses
appeared in F.D. Finlay's *Northern Whig* under the pen
name Coilus, and in 1859, he won second prize in the
Whig's competition for poems celebrating the centenary
of Robert Burns; a prize also went to Patrick Given of
Cullybackey, one of three writing brothers, the judge
being Professor George Lillie Craik (1798–1866) of the
Queen's College, Belfast, a prolific and popular author of
books on literary history and general information –
his bust is in the university's entrance hall. There are four
other compositions by Ulster writers in the large
anthology of *Burns Centenary Poems* (Glasgow 1859), one

of these being by 'Barney Maglone' (R.A. Wilson, 1820–1875), the once well-known journalist and Bohemian.

Flecher's first book, *Rhymes and Ravings of a County Antrim Lad* appeared anonymously in the same year. This, besides giving information which enables us to correct D.J. O'Donoghue's estimated birth-date for the poet, displays considerable evidence of his country schoolmastering. The first set of verses, 'The Irish Schoolmaster's Humble Petition', is the most explicit statement of the economic plight of the profession at that time, and several other poems deepen the gloom; 'The Aged Teacher', 'An Epistle to an Old Schoolmaster'. A couple of political pieces, on O'Connell and on Smith O'Brien, together with a number of historical ballads show his sympathies to have then been with the Irish nationalists. Perhaps it was realisation of the risk which the holding of such opinions entailed that delayed publication until even their anonymity should no longer prove dangerous. In the second volume, *Poems, Songs and Ballads* (1866), many of these were omitted, and while the mood was still nationalist, the expression had been tempered. Several of the ballads in the earlier book had a patriotic intention. 'The Outlaw's Dream' is very much in the manner of J.J. Callanan (1795–1829), one of the first Irish poets to write in a perceptibly Irish mode. And, in a number, Flecher's use of Irish words such as *saggan, canavan*, shows the first hint, in the north, of the Irish Literary Revival, thirty years later. Some of the Irishry, especially in the lyrics of his second volume, display evidence of the influence of Francis Davis (1810–1886), to whom *Rhymes and Ravings* had been dedicated, although the poets did not meet until Stewart brought them together in April 1868, not long before their visit to Huddleston.

The 1866 volume was Flecher's most representative, containing over two hundred pages of verse. A much later volume published in Chicago in 1900, *Odin's Last Hour and Other Poems*, even in its title-piece, draws upon the preceding collection. His material resources were extensive: 'The Giant's Ring' in Spenserian stanzas, 'Slieve Donard' in sound blank verse, sonnets on the Shakespearian pattern, the 'In Memoriam' quatrain popularised by the Poet Laureate. He even used Standard Habbie in standard English, and, again in straight English, modified *The Cherry and the Slae* quatorzain.

Though we might readily designate him as Provincial, there is a quality in his verse which links him to Samuel Ferguson, and casts a forward shadow to the poems of Ethne Carbery (Anne Johnston 1866–1902) and Alice Milligan (1866–1953), the Provincial reaching towards the recognisably National.

But his enduring awareness of the vernacular may be gauged from the word list at the end of the book, headed 'Glossary of Provincial Terms etc.', which goes to show the flexibility of labels in this field. Further, he swapped verse epistles with Huddleston and James McKowen in the traditional bardic manner, and was on good terms with David Herbison.

One definite gesture of community participation may be found in the lines, 'Why I signed the call to Rev D Thompson, Moneyreagh, Co. Down, December 1865', a batch of light verse in octosyllabic couplets, which salutes the new minister as:

> No reverend ass that brays and kicks
> At infidels and heretics;
> No zealot all on fire to sweep

Dissenters to the brimstone deep . . .
– while from pulpits, wide and far,
Sound the harsh notes of party war,
Rousing one race to hate another,
Till brother, maddened, murders brother,
You, you will quench these coals of hell
From charity's all-hallowed well . . .

But it is only in a number of songs in which the vernacular strikes an inevitable note and in the two considerable stanza-poems, 'May Day' and 'The Churn', rewritten and expanded from the straightforward narrative of 1859, that he stands shoulder to shoulder with the best of the rhymers. These lively pieces have, however, a County Antrim setting, drawn as they are from the experience of his youth near Lough Beg, but folk-customs ignored administrative limitations, and Flecher remains the best poet among those who taught school in County Down.

THE RURAL BARDS
of
COUNTY ANTRIM

I have already defined the country covered by the bards of south Antrim as very much the territory of John Dickey's subscribers in 1818, the valley of the Six Mile Water, the country of the book clubs, of Samuel Ferguson's specification. The County Down bards we tend to consider as isolated individuals: Hugh Porter never refers to Francis Boyle; Peter Burns and Robert Huddleston give no evidence of contact; Edward L. Sloan and William Bleakley do not seem to have heard of each other. But in south Antrim they cluster. James Campbell knew James Orr who was friendly with Samuel Thomson. Thomas Beggs, Orr's kinsman, knew Campbell and was a member of the Four Towns Book Club to which Thomson and Samuel Walker also belonged. Though John McKinley lived far to the north of the county, Beggs knew him, and both of them subscribed to Dickey's book. John Fullarton knew Beggs. Yet it was never in their tradition to hold a court or contest of the poets, as their Irish-speaking counterparts had done until the beginning of the century. Indeed, the last Gaelic bards' festival was held in 1826 at Dundalk.

James Campbell of Ballynure (1758–1818) has some claim to be thought the typical folk-poet. Fullarton, who wrote Beggs' biography, composed a sketch of him, too. From this we learn that he was born in the parish of Cairncastle, was taught to write a firm easy hand and had a fair acquaintance with figures. Learning the weavers' trade, he moved to Ballynure, as a journeyman working in several places adjacent. He married, settled in Ballynure village and had seven children. After a while he moved to the townland of Ballybracken. As a United Irishman, he was arrested in 1798, and had his papers seized by the authorities, these comprised of all his verses to date; and, on his release, they were not returned; the fate of how many modern Russian poets? He died in 1818, and was accorded a Masonic funeral on a big scale. It was to benefit his widow and children that the *The Posthumous Works* was published two years later, but it aggregated fewer than three hundred subscribers. He was of dark complexion, middle stature, of firm build, very active in youth and personally brave. As Fullarton records, 'Copies of his songs were sent as soon as written off to friends who stood first in Campbell's estimation; and thus passed into a local popularity; while his society was everywhere welcomed; especially at drinking parties, where he was sure to hear those songs chanted in full chorus.' Of his opinions, Fullarton states that 'a species of hostility to the upper ranks is at times manifested in his pieces. He considered that he owed no gratitude to the wealthy men of the world.'

After his death, when the manuscripts were being gathered in for the book, Alexander McDowell, a schoolmaster of some literary pretensions, 'judiciously suppressed' some of them. As the same gentleman performed a like service for Orr's work of 1817, we must wonder what has been lost in both instances. Certainly he seemed to have preferred insipid English to the sturdy vernacular. 'The Irish Cottier's Death and Burial' is the only piece in that volume he put in. Apart from this, the best of Orr is the other book which he himself saw printed. So we may be a little surprised that Campbell's couplet survived:

> Who make the rich? The answer's sure,
> It must be the industrious poor . . .

At any rate love for his songs and rhymes lingered on in the community, until John Corry felt the need for a re-issue of *Poems and Songs* (Ballyclare, 1870). And my own copy of the original volume has had a multitude of readers, the eager, not always well-washed, hands almost tearing it to bits, its covers patched with a grocer's calendar.

Campbell's cynical estimate of the Rebellion, as given in 'Willie Wark's Song':

> In 98 we armed again
> To right some things that we thought
>   wrang;
> We got so little for our pains
> It's no' worth mindin' in a song . . .

might well have received Orr's approval, for he too was out in the Rebellion. Born in 1770, a weaver and the son of a weaver, he had contributed verse to the *Northern Star*, the journal of the United Irishmen founded in 1792 in Belfast, where the society had been started the year before. Orr's 'Donegore Hill' in *The Holy Fair* stanza, a gnarled poem, closely worked in Scots, tells of the hosting of the pikemen before marching on Antrim for the battle. In 'The Prayer written on the Eve of the

Unfortunate 7th June 1798' occurs the quatrain:

> But in the victory or the rout,
> In glory or in gall,
> May moderation mark my power
> And fortitude my fall.

After the defeat and scattering – Orr has another set
of verses, 'The Execution' on the hanging of a rebel from
a tree – he went as the phrase has it 'on his keeping' in
the vicinity of Slemish mountain with his leader, Henry
Joy McCracken, and the remnant of his force. The poem,
'The Wanderer', must have taken its inspiration from
some such circumstance. He was apparently caught at
last and brought to Carrickfergus gaol. As testimony
to Orr's humane behaviour during the battle was forth-
coming, he was allowed to go into exile, to America.
'The Passengers' describes the voyage in vigorous Scots,
a forceful evocation of the crossing, and ends with the
disembarkation in the strange new land:

> Creatures wha' neer had seen a black
> Fu' scar't took to their shankies;
> Sae, wi' our best rags on our back,
> We mixt among the Yankies,
> An' skailt, that day.

We may think of that other poet, Donagh
Macnamara, County Clare, who made the voyage ear-
lier in the century and wrote, in Irish, a 'Mock Aeneid'
of it; for comparison of the two poems might suggest
one or two of the deep differences between the 'Two
Nations' which some are now seeking to define.

Though Orr stayed long enough to have some pieces
in an American newspaper and have them noticed, in

some months, we cannot say how many, he returned home to resume his work, where he found that his father was on the point of death, the father he later elegised:

> He strove to form my taste and heart,
> My hand he trained without a rod,
> And bade me, void of self and art
> Befriend my race and love my God.

To his old friend Sam Thomson, whose sympathies had been with the other side of the Rebellion, he addressed an epistle in *The Cherry and the Slae* stanza:

> For me, wi' a' that's come an' past
> I'm at my ain fireside at last
>   Fu' blythe, tho' fasht a wee,
> When geckt-at by the purse-proud drove: –
> But diel may care, sin' little love
>   Is lost 'tween them an' me.

Some suspicion of his loyalty to the civil authorities must have lingered on, for, when he applied to be allowed to join the Broadisland Infantry, a yeomanry corps founded about 1800, he was not accepted. This event provoked a song from James Campbell entitled 'The Rejected Yeoman'. But his friendship with Thomson was secure, as swapped and joint subscriptions show. At this time also he was contributing to the *Belfast Monthly Magazine*, the *Newsletter* and the *Chronicle*.

Orr's *Poems on Various Subjects* (1804) drew its 470 subscribers largely from his home area. From it he made little financial gain, but achieved some reputation. For example, he was invited by the Moravians of Gracehill, Ahoghill, to attend a complimentary dinner, an occasion he celebrated in verse. But he seems thereafter to have fallen into irregular habits, which his mastership of the

Masonic lodge he had founded in Ballycarry must have done little to modify. The death of his old mother deepened his gloom, as did his unrequited affection for a lady 'too far removed by social position from the sphere of life he occupied. Possessing none of the sweets of domestic enjoyment, he often flew the cheerless habitation of the bachelor, and was obliged to seek the pleasures of society at an inn', as McDowell has it, in his biographical sketch, echoing that pathetic stanza of William Shenstone:

> Whoe'er has travell'd life's dull round,
> Whate'er his stages may have been,
> May sigh to think he still has found
> The warmest welcome at an inn.

He died on 24 April 1816, and was buried in Templecorran Churchyard where there is a monument to his memory. An earlier desire that his verses should be seen through the press by two friends, and that, if any profit accrued, it should be distributed among the poor of the parish, resulted in the publication of *The Posthumous Works* of 1817, with that brief sketch of his life by McDowell, and the loss of we cannot tell how many lively verses. The *Belfast Penny Journal* described him as 'of a stature rather low, but well formed; his cheeks were ruddy and his eyes expressive and lively'. John Fullarton in the *Ulster Magazine*, May 1801, gives another, slightly different view, 'He was of middle stature, slightly stooped, with hair a pale chestnut colour. His voice was slow and he spoke broad Scotch till his death.' But the *Belfast Literary Journal*, 29 April 1816, in its obituary of this 'self-taught rural bard' has more relevance to the verses, when it saluted him 'as warm, generous, social-hearted'.

Frequently throughout the last century and well into this, Orr's poem 'The Irishman', which begins:

> The savage loves his native shore,
> Though rude the soil and chill the air,
> Then well may Erin's sons adore
> Their isle, which Nature formed so fair . . .

appeared in anthologies of Anglo-Irish verse, the most recent known to me being John Cooke's *Dublin Book of Irish Verse* 1728–1909 (new impression 1924). The sentimental patriotism and the rhetorical English of this single item have been fatally effective in diverting attention from his fine quality and significance. Often his English verses are competent, but seldom more than that. It is in the vernacular, the Scots pieces, that his considerable strength lies. 'The Penitent' and 'The Irish Cottier's Death and Burial' are far beyond the capacity of any other of our rural rhymers, in firmness of structure and consistency of language, undoubtedly the major successes in scale in our vernacular literature. 'Donegore Hill' and 'The Passengers' also, though of more limited aim, are without parallel. Indeed, handling his native idiom, he seems unable to go wrong. He could not, however, strike the lyrical note of Boyle's 'Bonny Weaver', Campbell's 'Molly Hume' or Beggs' 'Slievie Trew', for he seemed to lack the light response at the instant; rather, he laid his subject on the bench of his mind and brought to its expression the three great Scots stanza forms which he manipulated with a craftsman's authority. Among the more spontaneous, less self-conscious rural bards we find little awareness of the problems of diction; they grabbed the words which lay around them or snatched their rhymes from the crowd at the fair or 'the singing'. The dilemma involved in writing for any other audience than that on the inn-benches or around the hearth never troubled them. But Orr, clearly a deeper thinker, who looked at his words before using them – remember, he was slow of speech – faced it frankly:

My rude Scotch rhymes the tasteful justly slight,
The Scotch-tongued rustics scorn each nobler
    flight . . .

We can only guess what veins of irony inform that couplet, for one who 'spoke broad Scotch till his death', but had gentlemen riding out from Belfast to see the self-taught rustic bard for themselves.

Campbell, for one, essayed no noble flight. 'The Epicure's Address to Bacon' and 'The Landladies' Address to Bacchus', while rich in social content, do not present either classical properties or express the allegiances of the spirit, though his 'Dirge written at the grave of Orr' has a simple dignity in its unadorned octosyllables. Campbell never attempted the density of texture in Orr's 'rude Scotch rhymes' or the attempted decorum of his standard English. In fact most of his vernacular quality lies in the local pronunciation of the words, sound rather than shape. For his lyrics, he seems to display familiarity with current broadsheets, or hawkers' ballads, in the use of repeated internal rhyme or assonance. It may well be, owing to the circumstances of the gathering-up of his uncollected papers on the writing-down of verses from the recollection of friends for *The Posthumous Works*, items have crept into the canon to which his name should not be affixed, or it may be, with the nonchalance of the folk-singer, he caught something overheard and strung it into a fabrication of his own.

Though eight years younger than Campbell and four years older than Orr, Samuel Thomson (1766–1816) cannot be considered as standing between them in any sort of gradation. They were weavers; he was a schoolmaster. Born near Templepatrick, he lived in a cottage on the north side of Lylehill, in the townland of Carngranny, which he called Crambo Cave. For his first volume, *Poems on Different Subjects* (Belfast, 1793), dedicated to 'Mr Robert Burns the celebrated Ayrshire poet', he secured about 350 subscriptions chiefly from the Antrim and Belfast areas, but with half a dozen for Dublin and a full dozen for Boston, USA. The two local book clubs of Doagh took copies. William Magee took ten, another Belfast bookseller, John Hughes, twenty-five. Hughes was later to become known as an informer inside the Society of United Irishmen. That society was further represented by Henry Joy McCracken, by Samuel Neilson and Bartholomew Teeling, and two lower-ranking members were Luke Mullan of the Four Towns Book Club, and James Orr, at this date designated Junior, his father still living. In the second volume, *New Poems* (1799), the 1798 Rebellion supervening, this radical support was withdrawn largely by execution or exile.

For this he had about three hundred subscribers, mostly drawn from County Antrim and Belfast, with Nicholas Grimshaw, one of the new industrialists, and Samuel Luke, a frequent subscriber to local verse, of any note among them. *Simple Poems* (1806) did better, reaching six hundred; Ballynure Book Club and Killead Literary Society, with Orr, long since back from his American sojourn, and Luke again, and the 'Dante' Boyd, with another Boyd, David this time, a Belfast schoolmaster who wrote the very flat-footed *Poor House*

(1806). Largely the area of support was much the same, with rather more from north Down than for the earlier book.

The pedantic attitude of the schoolmaster with literary ambitions emerges from the 'Preface to the Indulgent Reader': 'Burns erected an edifice, that, defying the tooth of time, will stand for ages. My weakly constructed hovel, like the *shiel* of the Caledonian shepherd, in a season or two must moulder beneath the crushing foot of the hoary traveller'; and, though reckoned only second to Orr, his reputation faded in a few years, and does not reappear in the record until, in his 1844 collection, Huddleston printed an 'Elegy' to his memory of some two hundred lines which displays a wide knowledge of the work. Careful to point out that his Thomson was 'not the Season's Bard' with a precision that Sam would have approved, he indignantly denounced the injustice of fate:

> Shall Burns be dress'd in garbs the best,
> And Ramsey blossom in the urn,
> And Ferguson fame's noblest boast
> And Thompson meet no fond return?

Reading these lines, the fleeting image crosses my mind of those pocket-size editions bound in tartan covers, on sale at the birthplace at Alloway, and another thought that the Bard of Moneyreagh might have spelled the old poets' names correctly. These are but flickers across the screen, the tenor of the communication is clear. Admitting that he had never known him,

> I who was not in embryo,
> Nor then had drunk the natal air,

– this might help us to establish Huddleston's date of birth: certainly post 1816 – with liberal references to the poet's themes and their excellences – 'His Odes are in the unrivall'd class' – he gently urges:

> Accept this humble tribute paid
> And hear a bard esteem thy lays.

And one will recognise the sincerity in this salute of a younger to an elder within the same tradition, the feeling of kinship, the sense of ancestry, the fear of the same fate, and the challenge on behalf of the elder which embodies that of the younger, also, when his turn comes to be forgotten. In a prose note to the elegy, Huddleston states his claim: 'To have an accurate idea of his merit, the reader must inquire at his productions', which is all that any poet asks, for his own work.

Thomson is of altogether a more literary cast of mind than any of the other schoolmasters of Antrim or Down who were his contemporaries. In his first book he sets out a stanza of impressive names:

> Homer I've read and Virgil too,
> With Horace, Milton, Young and Gay,
> Auld Spencer, Pope and Dryden thro',
> Sweet Thomson, Shenstone, Goldsmith, Gray . . .

an asterisk to the first name specifying 'translations only'. He was able to show some discrimination in his reading, as another stanza demonstrates:

> Tho' Allan Ramsay blithly ranted
> An' tun'd his reed wi' merry glee,
> Yet, faith that *something* ay he wanted
> That makes my Burns so dear to me.

We find Sylvanders, Edwins, Damons, Davys, Betseys and Simkins in plenty, who have flitted through the pastorals of more than one century. He was able to imitate the styles of Ramsay, Fergusson and Burns in an eclogue. He knew of Bruce, of Beattie, and John Cunningham, that sadly neglected but excellent minor poet we have not yet found a crevice for in Anglo-Irish literature, despite his Dublin birth.

As an example of his cultural ostentation, one might quote from 'Lyle's Hill – A Rhapsody':

> O had I Denham's classic skill,
> Or Dyer's soft descriptive quill,
> The beauties of verdant Lyle
> Should echo round my native isle . . .
> Great Pope had Windsor's lofty groves . . .
> O how I love to lie, sweet Lyle,
> Upon the grassy brow the while
> Dan Phoebus drinks the morning dew
> Ascending up from Slavy-true . . .

This is some distance from the vocabulary of the weavers and begs attention from those who recognise the place of Cooper's Hill, Windsor Forest and Grongar Hill in the development of the 'Prospect Poem' of Augustan literature. It is also of interest in the light of the fact that this kind of poem, of description of landscape with a varying focus, was very slow in emerging in the verse-books of this island, William Carr's *Rosstrevor* (Newry, 1810) being the earliest northern example. But, for Thomson, the insistent vernacular which was spoken around him and found in that other literature with which he was familiar, asserts itself in 'Davie and Sawney', an ale-house eclogue:

> 'Twas on a snell October mornin',
> When contra' folk had a' their corn in;
> An' northern hills began to shaw
> Their healthy summits white wi' snaw . . .

And something kindles within the verse, a breath of actuality, and when he contemplates his 'boor-tree, chaplain – like to all', a certain verbal wit finds its place in an exercise in Standard Habbie:

> Here blithe beneath thy auld grey branches,
> Where sparrows chirp and spotted finches,
> Prepare for their companion wenches
>   The nest well feather'd,
> I bind my wild flowers up in bunches
>   That I hae gather'd.

The vernacular is light, but the traditional stanza-mould is firm enough to contain the word-play.

A countryman as well as a pedagogue, he carries some measure of weather-lore, as in 'To a Robin Red-Breast':

> Among the many properties
> Delightful bird! thou'rt weather wise,
>   And by thy song we know
> Whether we'll have a shining day,
> Or drizzling, wet and windy fray,
>   As thou art high or low.

Away from books then, his observation can be exact:

> The lapwing wallops o'er the bogs . . .

or when he invites us in 'July', during the turf-cutting season, to:

See, side-wide on suggans, the turf driving boors . . .

though that last noun brings back the book-mastered accent of his dominie's vocabulary. But the full armouring of his observation, wit, and folk-consciousness, comes to the peak in his 'To a Hedgehog', certainly his finest, most concentrated effort.

His honest appraisal of his own physical, domestic circumstance is seen in an epistle to a friend who failed to visit him:

> It was not worth your while;
> To sup on buttermilk and slugs
> And lie on chaffy hammock,
> Beneath our coarse-grained country rugs
> Would suit but ill your stomach.

sharpens the dichotomy between reality and the ideal of the pastoral. He will take off, at the drop of a literary name or anything that might prompt his feet to leave the ground, as in the 'Verses' addressed to Mrs Thomson of the hermitage:

> Shenstonian fire thy bosom warm'd
> With all his Leasowes-sketching glow
> And to see this curious grotto form'd
> His genius hover'd down below

Yet against this dream of aesthetic elegance we can set a brutal epigram, a coarse description of snuff-taking, or an indelicate attack on Thomas Paine – 'poor wasp of commotion, the football of fate' – being the least objectionable line in it – and the consequent tensions now and then achieve a momentary resolution, in the unsentimental recollection, say, of Halloween:

In pairs, before the ingle now
The mystic nits are laid alang
And blink and burn, some right some wrong,
And social grannie taks her smoke
Laughs wi' the lave, an' clubs his joke
Gies her auld mou' the youthfu' twine
Waesucks, to think on a' lang syne
And tells how happy she has been
A-burning nits on Halloween.

Campbell, Orr and Thomson were dead before John Dickey's *Poems on Various Subjects* (1818) appeared, and, after them, he seems something of a foot-soldier, a step or two to the rear. His book has an epistle to Thomson, May 1813. A second, dated November 1814, and a subsequent set of rhymes, make clear that he had met the older bard and had been lent one of his books. The final item of the group laments Thomson's death. In August 1812, Dickey wrote to Orr whom he had not met, reporting that he had heard 'You like a glass' and eulogising his poems; compared to him Dickey feels himself 'a rhyming block head blether'. The verses are in the same stanza as Orr's 'Donegore Hill' to which reference is made, a thoughtful compliment since they were addressed from that very place. He sent verses to Orr announcing Thomson's death, and completes the florilegium of friendship with a later elegy when Orr died.

Dickey has too much dull diction-laden verse in standard English and on set themes. His best poems are in the vernacular; two of them, in particular, are of sociological interest. 'Country Singin'' tells of the open air singing games young men and women played, and 'A Rural Colloquy' recounts in dialogue the domestic activities of a Saturday evening, the weekly shaving of the men, the women's washing of the clothes and baking the bread.

Among his poetically listed subscribers, Dickey names, you remember, 'poet McKinley of Dervock'. This cannot be other than John McKinley who put 'Dunseveric' after his name on the title-page of his *Giant's Causeway* (1819). His second Dublin-printed book gives him no territorial appellation. It may have been that, since Dunseverick has a ruined castle and was that much nearer to the Causeway, it gave some imagined right to, or authority for, treatment of that theme. At any rate, McKinley presents a somewhat enigmatic figure.

Beggs in his *The Rhyming Pedagogues* (1821) saluted the genuine poets of his time as James Orr, William McComb – that sanctimonious bookseller, 'the Laureate of Presbyterianism' and much else – Robert Anderson, and John McKinley, but later made an odd reference to him as fond of 'his jug, his pipe, his w—e'. For an uncouth, unlettered, 'I was only six months at school' swain, McKinley manages the heroic couplet, both in 'The Causeway' and the fragmentary 'The Traveller Benighted in Mourne', competently but without distinction and with a ready use of the eighteenth-century lexicon – 'refrigeration's gelid power' and so on, showing once in a while the influence of Oliver Goldsmith, whom he names after Robert Bloomfield and Robert Burns, as the third poet in the progress of his poetic education. Though parts of his 'The Causeway' were written before he had perused the Reverend William Hamilton Drummond's which had come out in 1811, nevertheless, he feels that any hint of indebtedness should be admitted forthwith, so he begins:

> Genius of Erin! in my native clime,
> Where Drummond's harp awoke the strain
>   sublime . . .

But, by comparison with the little doctor's well-cargoed work, his poem is not of much interest. 'The Traveller Benighted', with the cottage welcome of:

> With modest guise the infant group retire
> To let the bashful stranger share the fire . . .

and its invocation to the still actively patronising members of the Dromore circle, has much more life and variety. The last passage:

> All hail ye patrons of the hapless bard,
> From whom e'en weakest merit meet reward;
> Where lovely Hilltown looks o'er silver Bann
> That laves Rathfriland, winds through Moneyslan,
> See classic Boyd and philanthropic Tighe
> Disclaim the pride of scornful scrutiny,
> Protect and patronise the rustic lay,
> And usher drooping genius into day . . .

was well-directed: 'Dante' Boyd and the helpful editor of the Bard of Moneyslan were among his subscribers, and, surely, recruited the incumbent Bishop Thomas Percy of Dromore, and Thomas Stott and Mr Hugh Porter himself, not an Esquire, this time, but the best of the book is in the vernacular verses, the fine 'A Winter Night in the North of Ireland' and several other pieces in Standard Habbie, well-handled, including a touching poem 'To a Redbreast', restricted to only three stanzas. We find him inhabiting a world in which a childhood friend is press-ganged for the navy, and an eccentric clergyman-

antiquary assembles a remarkable collection of odd-
ments. The latter is the subject of some gentle fun, but
did not fail to join the subscribers.

In the Dublin printed book of 1821, 'The Causeway'
is shorn of one hundred lines, but 'The Traveller
Benighted', with a new subtitle of 'A Retrospect of
O'Neill', has been lengthened to take in an anapaestic
invocation and a page or two of octosyllables on the
inserted, historic theme. All the rest, bad and good, has
been cut out. Of course we have examples of some of
our country bards being rather apologetic for the ver-
nacular, and we have instances of busybody editors
removing the offending material, but I know of no other
poet of this kind silently disowning his own best, most
authentic work.

Beggs must have met McKinley first on his walking
tour round the north coast of Antrim which provided
the experience and material for his poem, *Rathlin; A
descriptive poem, written after a visit to that island* (1820).
Otherwise variously designated Beggs of Hilltown, of
Ballyclare, of Cottonmount, we know a fair amount
about his history, but his bibliography is somewhat com-
plicated, owing to the existence of revised editions and
the absence of dates for the books and the little booklets
which appeared of his verse from 1819 to 1844. Only
David Herbison had a longer career of publication, but
then he lived to be a very much older man.

Beggs, saluted by James McKowen as

> Wizard minstrel! sweet and wild,
> Self taught genius, nature's child,

and by Herbison as

> The sweetest bard
> The vales of Ulster ever knew,

died in 1847, but his reputation had retained sufficient momentum for Samuel Corry in 1867 to bring out an edition of his poems in four paper-backed parts, with later, a bound edition of these, buttressed with the bio-graphical preface by John Fullarton.

Beggs was born in Glenwhirry which lies on the northern slopes of the rural bards' territory, in 1789. His father was a farm-labourer, his mother a first cousin of James Orr. In 1794 the family moved to Whiteabbey on the shore of Belfast Lough, and while living there, Beggs as a boy went to sea in a coasting vessel. But after a ship-wreck near Rathlin, and in response to his mother's appeal, he returned home. Later the family moved to Ballyclare where his father became tenant of a small farm until his death in 1821. While living at Ballyclare Beggs secured employment in a local bleachworks. His first book, *Miscellaneous Pieces in Verse*, was printed by F.D. Finlay in 1819. He must have been writing hard for some years for, in his preface, he remarks, 'After propos-ing to publish a Work of 170 pages at three shillings price, then suffering it to dwindle into the present size, some kind of apology may be required; and that which I now offer, is – want of liberal patronage . . . I have still the manuscript in my possession which would form a larger volume than the one proposed . . .' Of the twenty-nine items in this book only thirteen are includ-ed in Corry's posthumous selection.

Shortly after this, the opportunity arose for him to become agent for a Belfast linen firm in France, but this fell through, and Beggs found himself out of work. It was then, while disengaged, that he set out on his north Antrim walking tour. The next year *Rathlin* appeared – and in the year following – *The Rhyming Pedagogue*, with its critical sketches, in the vein of:

> Now Wilson comes, a flimsy fool,
> The tyrant of his hedge-hut school.

Among the other poems in the booklet an elegy on James Orr gives us some useful information on his kinsman's career, specifying that, 'on the run' after the Battle of Antrim:

> Where Slemish lifts his barren head
> Enamoured of the nipping air',
> Beneath the herdsman's hearth-less shed,
> The smile of mercy met him there
> And purple Collin's healthy height
> And Wherry's fairy-haunted glen,
> Have often seen the luckless wight,
> Like felon, seek a secret den ...

During this period, Beggs seems to have tried to live by writing, relying upon his widowed mother for food and shelter, but in 1825 he obtained regular employment in a bleachworks at Cottonmount, not far from Belfast. He married a couple of years later, and in 1828, brought out *The Momento, a Choice Variety of Original Poems*. His prose, *Nights in a Garret*, came in 1830, and includes a description of a country book club of which he had been a member for some time, Hightown or 'Hay Town', as he calls it, otherwise the Four Towns Book Club. F.J. Bigger drew upon this for the article I have already mentioned.

He then found another job in a bleach and print works at Ardoyne, Belfast. Here, in 1834, he published *The Minstrel's Offering*. This was well received, but he shortly fell out of work once more, and, with his family of five, found haven with his only brother who also gave shelter to their aged mother. In 1836 Beggs issued the *Second Part of the Minstrel's Offering*, nearly twice as bulky as the first, priced one shilling. Eight years later, a revised and enlarged edition of *Rathlin* came from the same printer, Hugh Clarke. He contributed verse to the *Belfast Penny Journal*, the *Newsletter* and the *Banner of Ulster*. All this, with renewed engagement to his former employers at Cottonmount, where he found 'a neat cottage standing on the bank of a solitary stream, surrounded by trees and cultivated fields', suggests something of an Indian summer for the bard, for by now he was saluted by a younger generation like Herbison and McKowen, but in July 1847 he died during one of the epidemics of that tragic time, and no stone was raised to mark his grave at Ballylinny, near Ballyclare.

Fullarton writes of Beggs' 'improvidence', and 'want of personal energy and fortitude', but for a frequently unemployed man with the burden of a family to stick to the craft of verse and steer so much of it into print, though 'to this child of song the hand of patronage was never once extended through his literary struggles', would argue some persistence and confidence in his talent. 'In person he was about middle height, of slender make and delicate constitution, his features pale and intellectual.' In his elegy Herbison wrote:

> 'Twas thine to walk in sorrow's way,
> Sweet child of sensibility!
> Except thine own loved Sabbath day,
> No day of rest appeared for thee,
> Hard labour, penury, and pain
> Still held thee in their iron chain!

Because of the nature of his employment and the fact

that he followed it in several places, Beggs had nothing of the rooted, local quality of the other rural bards. So we look in vain among his verses for those celebrations of occasion, the rituals which mark the season, like the Harvest Churn, the May Eve or Halloween customs. He is seldom the community articulate. Consequently, though he asserted that he used 'the language of his native glen', this was much modified by his change of residence, until it became a more generalised instrument, only lightly flecked with strong indigenous words. He considered that it might be 'supposed that in some places (he) had imitated the Scottish dialect'. Although he was writing for a dispersed reading public, not for the lads and lassies at the crossroads, and knew well enough that his idiom was far from fully-charged, but to the eye of a stranger might look like Scots, he wished to establish that he had a right to the forms he used. He never used the great Scots stanzas, whereas the rooted bard could hardly fail to shape his thoughts in word-patterns which fitted them. He wrote his epistle to Herbison in octosyllabic couplets, Herbison replied in Standard Habbie. The vernacular was changing, was in the process of becoming looser, less vigorous. With these altering circumstances his lyrical talent gave utterance to emotions and moods which arose from the human condition in the drive or drift of the change, as in his 'Auld Wife to her Wheel' or 'The Wee Pauper Wean', and though a well-read man who knew his Young, Pope, Gray, Thomson and Falconer, he was not gripped by the obsolete authority of a poetic diction.

Reading his verse we miss the gusto of Boyle or Huddleston. He has none of the well-based strength of Orr, able to construct on it poems which are both concentrated and large-scaled. There is a harsh note, too, in some of his predecessors, but his store of general gloom had no proud individual cry of protest, rather instead a kind of sentimental self-pity. Francis Davis has, to my ear, a hint of it: neither Campbell nor Orr, though they had their personal griefs, had it. It may well have been due to a collective social mood, compounded of the decline in the status of the country bard, as rural life became bleaker, drained by emigration, in the grim atmosphere of the forties.

We might compare him with Samuel Walker (1803–1885) who had been a fellow-member of the Four Towns Book Club. He lived at Shaneshill, near Templepatrick, and, though he contributed a small handful of poems and some prose to Belfast journals, he never had a book printed; all that we are now left with is a manuscript notebook in the Bigger Collection of the Belfast Public Library. This seems to consist of verses made in the decade 1829–1839, and, markedly unlike his few printed verses, though one of these is 'The Churn; or the Last Day of Harvest', are in a dense vernacular. He used Standard Habbie fluently and frequently:

> Their number now is unco' sma'
> Wha credit fairie tales ava;
> The fairie forths are plantit a'
> Wi' groves a timmer,
> Or else they carry craps fu' braw
> O' corn in simmer.

His 'Wake' is in *The Holy Fair* stanza, crammed with folk usage and belief:

> Then let's suppose the e'en to close,
> O' some auld bed-rid neighbour,

> The frien's maun then, 'ts a rule ye ken,
> A while refrain frae labour.
> To tapster Jack's wi' jars in sacks,
> As fast as they can bicker,
> Twa sturdy chiels scour 'cross the fields
> For two-three kin's o' liquor
>   For the Wake that Night.

With the coming of the 'corpse-dresser', who is 'hanselt wi' a facer', or given a sustaining drink before tackling the grim task, sews up the shroud and lays out the body on a bed 'bedeckt wi' linen':

> An' through some freet, o' saut a plate
> Is placed upo' its belly

The passage-rites are recorded in like detail – these are followed by a lighter-hearted stanza of some verve:

> Auld wifes their wheels, their rocks an' reels,
> Throw by like things disgustin',
> An' may be seen in shaw an' sheen,
> Fast neist the wake house postin',
> While young anes fair sleek up their hair,
> An' trig themsets fu' brawly,
> For they expeck that at the wake
> They'll meet a hale travallie
> O' boys that night.

At this point the metrical pattern switches suddenly to that of *The Cherry and the Slae*. Even the four-foot couplet, given a feminine last foot, in his hands keeps a vernacular liveliness and authenticity, as on the lines for 'the death of a respected friend':

> Nae rack rent landlord there shall tease him,
> No churchman for his tenth stook seize him,
> No turnpike yett are there to stop him
> No dick dare there for fourpence kepp him . . .

But certainly the most idiosyncratic set of verses in this 157-page notebook is the 'Epistle to Hawkie the Cotter's Cow on hearing she had eaten the Bible'. Of this Walker declares that he only wrote between a dozen and twenty interspersed verses, the rest, and the whole plan being the work of his friend, William McNeice. This is an overlong and at times, monotonous piece, but now and then – we query: Are these Walker's interpolations? – neat and amusing points are made:

> Some folk will say thou wast to faut
> To be so greedy on the saut,
> But Hawkie, never think o' that
>   But flisk thy tail,
> An' say thou teuk the wife o' Lot
>   To saut thy kail.

> On Leah next thous try'd thy mettle
> That's blin's a cleg or pratto beetle,
> Jacob's he-goats an' spotted cattle,
>   Queer pye-bald beastie,
> Wi' monie a half-peel'd hazel wattle
>   Thou eat like peas strae . . .

Such verses could only emerge from a community where knowledge of the Bible was deep and general, and, specifically, in a pocket of that community where it was not treated with awe, but with a wry affection.

Although Walker had just enough literary ambition to

have his prose story of Eneas O'Haughan, the County Antrim highwayman, printed in the *Dublin Penny Journal* in 1836, he seems to have remained content to keep his notebook and add verses to it; in this too, he describes himself as 'a man of little sense and less wealth but who is fond of committing his stray thoughts to writing and if any of his simple neighbours are pleased with it all his labour is not lost', a succinct and humble definition of the plea and function of the folk-poet.

Another poet without a book to his name, James McKowen (1814–1889) seems to have had a steadier working life than most of his contemporaries. After a brief schooling, he found work with Barbours of Hilden, thread-manufacturers, and then, for forty years, at the Glenview bleachworks of Richardson Sons and Owden, from which, as I have earlier remarked, he retired on a pension.

Perhaps he was lucky in his employers, and, in himself, a steady man. He contributed verse to the *Nation*, that famous journal, under the pen name Curlew, and was also well known as Kitty Conner, his pseudonym in other journals, being particularly esteemed for his humorous song 'The Ould Irish Jig'. One of his lyrics, not the best, lasted in the anthologies until this century; but, in 1869, Ralph Varian's *The Harp of Erin* (Dublin) had as many as nine of them. Linguistically he is in much the same class as Beggs, using only a very light tincture of vernacular, but unlike Beggs, sometimes turning towards a sort of 'stage-Irish brogue', as might be expected from so fervent a lover of the playhouse with its period melodramas and farces. Incidentally, Hugh Leslie Stewart once wrote a song for a girl to sing in her act in the Belfast Music Hall; she reported afterwards, that 'it went down immense'.

McKowen seems, in the bardic fashion, to have exchanged verses with everybody from Beggs to Herbison, to have been a popular person, on visiting terms with many – this may have been due, in some measure, to the improved travelling facilities brought about by better roads and the introduction, in his life-time, of the steam-train, for he never lived in any area closely populated by the poets. Indeed, it can be only because they thought of him as one of themselves that we may place him among them. His manuscripts he left with an antiquary-friend for ultimate publication, but the bundle of papers appears to have vanished:

> The Bard of Dunclug
> Stands six feet in his hose
> Has a finely formed head
> And an aquiline nose:

So wrote McKowen of his friend, David Herbison (1800–1880), who was the dominant poet of mid-Antrim, a prolific and long-productive writer. Herbison was born in Mill Street, Ballymena, where his father kept an inn. Ten years later his father purchased a small farm at Laymore, in the neighbourhood, which he held till his death in 1825. Delicate as a child, Herbison was totally blind up to his seventh year, when the sight of the left eye was restored. He went to school at eight and attend-ed for two years, and after that became a pupil at 'a writ-ing school', but only for three months. When he was about ten he heard some verses of Allan Ramsay's repeated, and, being deeply impressed for a long time, travelled to Belfast on foot to buy a copy with his first wages. After helping on the farm, he was, at fourteen, apprenticed to hand-loom weaving. From then on, until quite late in life, save for his Canadian adventure, he was employed at his trade. He finally became local agent for a Belfast linen firm.

In 1827, with a married brother and his family, Herbison emigrated to Canada. The vessel was wrecked in the St Laurence river, his brother's wife and child drowned. After a few months stay during which he lodged with another brother who had emigrated earlier, he returned to Ballymena. He married in 1830, and in the same year had his first verses printed in the *Northern Whig*. Thereafter large quantities of his work appeared in Ulster journals – in ten years the *Ballymena Observer* printed sixty pieces – and, sometimes, outside the province. These were periodically gathered up in volumes, in 1841, 1848, 1858, 1869, 1876, with the aid of subscribers: *Midnight Musings* (1848) had nearly five hundred, *Children of the Year* (1876) over eight hundred. In the end he left enough funds to have a collected edition of the five volumes and other single items accumulated by the way. This came out in 1883 and runs to three hundred pages of double columns; so Herbison is, by all odds, our most voluminous maker of verses.

He had a great capacity for friendship, particularly with brother-bards, exchanging epistles with Beggs in 1841, and with Huddleston and McKowen in 1875, elegising McKenzie, Beggs, McMullan and Fullarton, as the sad occasions arose, sending valedictory verses to Flecher in his leaving for America. One of his oldest friends was Samuel Corry, the editor of Beggs and Campbell. Samuel Ferguson sent him his books from Dublin as they came out.

Spontaneous and indefatigable rhymer, he penned election ballads, made a song for Tenant Right, and verses for a tenants' banquet to their landlord, struck off memorial lines for the tiler of his Masonic lodge and for a host of clergy, found rhymes for an advertisement for a general store – Alexander Black's of Bridge Street. Frequently, for he seems to have earned the ancient bardic right to gifts, we may note him thanking folk for such benefactions as a cart of peats, prints of butter, a goose, a pot of jam. Certainly he was, at many levels, not all of the deepest significance, a recorder of the external life of his folk, a reliable journeyman. Once or twice in his first book, we come on attempts at historical narratives, but he failed to persist in that line.

Reputed to have an eye for nature, and although, by his own declaration, much of his work was composed in the open air, his attitude to nature was conventional. Very seldom does he equal 'Summer Time' in immediacy and authenticity:

> The lapwing flutters round about,
> To wile us from her bield,
> Lights at our feet and cries peweet,
> Then flies far o'er the field.
>
> And gladly from the auld cow's back
> The magpie steals the hair,
> To clothe her nest, where she may rest,
> Beyond the schoolboys' snare.

A few similes suggest the range of sensory experience upon which he signally failed to draw: one of them is:

> Her face is turned pale as the churn-staff in simmer
> That hings on the clear thorn frae morning till
> e'en . . .

And only occasionally are there references to the imaginative lore of the folk:

And oft ere the sun dried the leaf on the tree
I have found the witch-wife sitting coldly by thee,
And watched while she cast her old blanket abroad
To sip up the dew from the daisy-clad sod.

His written language was preponderantly English, with, now and then, a dialect word to establish his sense. He used Standard Habbie extensively, both in English and vernacular, and many of his best pieces are in that mode; but he never essayed either of the two other great Scots stanzas.

So Herbison is in much the same position as Beggs, perhaps even more emphatically, for as a kind of leading literary figure, he was forced away into the printed pages of Belfast, Dublin, even London magazines and deflected from the task of the rural bard, to explore the mind and being of the community in its own idiom, with the consequent inevitable thinning of his language. Nevertheless, when, in August 1948, on a bus travelling from Ballymena to Cushendall, I was reading *The Snow Wreath*, his volume of 1869, I sat beside an old man who remembered his father pointing out the Bard of Dunclug to him, as they passed in the fair.

The rest of Herbison's contemporaries in mid-Antrim have nothing of the coherence of the south Antrim company, neither socially nor linguistically. John Smyth (1783–1854), popular in the newspapers under the pen name 'Magowan', never published a book, and died in America. John Getty (1781–1857) and John Given (1813–1883) were schoolmasters, and their work is of little interest. There was also Hugh McWilliams, another pedagogue, whose visit to Ballymena I have already quoted from.

Two ladies might be mentioned, but they are both

eccentric to the theme of rural verse. The only connecting threads, tenuous though they must be, are that Herbison knew both and wrote friendly verses to them. The first, the beautiful Elizabeth Willoughby Treacy of Brigadee (1821–1896), published her first volume, *Poems by Finola*, in 1851. These are usually in the historical vein of 'Exiles Far Away' or 'Song of the Irish Minstrel', of the literary movements to which she belonged, for she had been a contributor to the *Belfast Vindicator*, a Home-Rule repeal journal founded by Charles Gavan Duffy, shortly after to edit the *Nation*, to which Miss Treacy, as well as James McKowen and Francis Davis, her fellow-northerners, also sent verses. She married Ralph Varian of Cork, whose anthology, already mentioned, gave unprecedented representation to northern poets, not unlikely due to her influence.

The other lady, Ida White, wife of the proprietor of the *Ballymena Observer*, produced her two romantic volumes later in the century, in 1874 and in 1890, although a good deal of the material was written before 1870. As a republican, a freethinker, and, later an exile in Paris, she followed a rather unusual career for a Ballymena woman, for which a spell of imprisonment in Holloway, a public attack on the Czar of Russia, and some verses addressed to John Burns the dockers' leader, set the key; with such a story one cannot help feeling sorry that she was not a better poet. If we remember that of 'the young and beautiful Miss Treacy' Herbison wrote 'Her thoughts are fluid and refined', and that on 23 July 1874, Mrs Ida White and he took shelter from a thunderstorm at Portrush, we have only added minute strokes to the sketchy portraits of these remarkable if scarcely relevant ladies.

Our final consideration must be concentrated upon

Poems from College and Country by Three Brothers (1900),
not only on point of date, neatly marking the century,
but because it provides an excellent example of the con-
trast between the schoolmaster and the rural poet, all the
more pertinent since the three brothers involved were
from Cullybackey, in the Ballymena area. Patrick Given
(1837–1864) was a bright student, a medal-winner,
became pupil-teacher, a device of the time and later,
rather like an apprenticeship, on the method if not the
theory of Dr Dotheboys. He went to a teacher-training
college in Dublin, and thereafter passed to the recently
established Queen's College, Belfast. While there he won
one of twelve prizes in the *Northern Whig* Burns
Centenary Competition, when Flecher came second to
Thomas Henry. In the spring of 1864 he won first prize
in the same journal's Shakespeare Tercentenary. In both
instances Professor George Lillie Craik, his English
teacher, was judge. But Given died suddenly that
autumn. Samuel Fee Given (1845–1867), a younger
brother, also became a pupil-teacher, and, in due course,
in charge of Tullgrawley National School, a two-teacher
school in the neighbourhood where R.L. Russell, author
of *The Child and His Pencil* (1935), was later principal,
and Ian Cochrane, author of *A Streak of Madness* (1973),
a pupil. Samuel died of tuberculosis after a protracted ill-
ness. The third brother in the book, Thomas Given
(1850–1917) left school in the third class to work on the
farm, where, with an interval of one or two years trying
his fortune in America, since, there, another, older bro-
ther was making progess in the legal profession, Thomas
remained on the farm for the rest of his life. He became
an active Freemason, secretary of his lodge for twenty-
five years, and, later, a Justice of the Peace.

Poems from College and Country with its list of 280

subscribers, and a new category of guarantors, many of whom are on the other list, appears to have been launched by Thomas the survivor, pulling all the strings of influence. The subscribers are strongly local, including fourteen Justices of the Peace, doctors, clergymen, among them the Moderator and past Moderator of the Presbyterian Church, and a block of over forty names from Philadelphia where Marcus, now deceased, had been prominent at the bar. The frontispiece is a photograph of the clergyman who wrote the biographical notices, and there is a dedication to and a full page portrait of the Provincial Deputy Grand Master of the Antrim Freemasons. With becoming modesty the photograph of Thomas is after page 136.

The thirty-two poems by Patrick are all in standard English, sentimental lyrics like 'Never forget a kindness', or invocations like 'The Spirit of Poesy', 'To a Nightingale' (there are, of course, no nightingales in Ireland), 'Ode to Eloquence' and a long blank-verse essay in which two educated young men argue their philosophies. His favourite poets, the writer of the biographical sketch declares, were Tennyson and Whittier. I should have thought Longfellow a more potent influence. Samuel, among his three-dozen pieces, has only one 'Drinking Song' which carries a whiff of the rural speech, and one pseudo-Irish effort about a 'swate little sowl'; the rest are banal rhymes and rhythms, 'Life Thoughts', 'Absence', 'The First False Step', commonplace in idea and conventional in imagery, showing no foothold in the soil or circumstance of the writer's life as countryman and schoolmaster.

But with Thomas's eighty rhymes the difference is marked. He could knock off album-verses, flimsy patriotic ballads on the faraway Boer War, the Defence of

Ladysmith, Buller's defeat at Colenso, hollow quatrains on the late Earl of Beaconsfield, light-handed tasks in which the whole man is not engaged. In his own preface he remarks that 'Many of the following trifles . . . have been sketchily committed to my note-book in the shelter of some unhearing hedge or in the ridges of my fields while at the plough.' And his biographer, the Reverend George R. Buick, declares:

> He is specially happy when using the Doric of his native district. Here his muse seems most at home, becoming at once more natural and forcible and employing, with spontaneity and freshness, language which is decidedly more idiomatic and picturesque than when he contents himself with dipping into "the well of English undefiled", whilst his rhythm is felt to be 'more crisp and sparkling, more instinct with subtle power and more unmistakably melodious.

One could hardly have put it more effectively. Not for him 'the little brown bird of the wandering wing' of his brother's nightingale; instead:

The blackbird keeks out frae the fog at the broo,
Gies his neb a bit dicht on a stane

which resists easy translation. Not for him a rhapsodic Spirit of Poesy, but vigorous lines on instrumental music in church, a divisive issue of the time. For him 'The Auld School at the Pun'', not college exercises. He is at home on his own ground, alert to defend his fellow tenant farmers, to celebrate the brotherhood of the lodge. He may even, when called upon, speak for the weavers on strike: all of these in Standard Habbie, or, favourite with him, *The Holy Fair*, the stanza with the bob-wheel, confidently handled, taken as the tools of the verse-making craft when the stuff to be worked is vernacular.

Yet, reading his pages, we are aware, I believe, that somewhere the centrality of the bard to his life and his community has broken down. It is a small point, but significant, that though he lived in the same part of the county and their years overlapped, it was only a book by the dead Bard of Dunclug which he saluted. He swapped no rhymes with fellow-poets, or, if he ever did, kept none as worth sharing. Nor does he ever glance at another man's trade with an informed, amused or affectionate eye.

His language still has more density and grain than Herbison's. But he has little of the intelligence and weight of a James Orr, or the muscle and sinew of a Francis Boyle or a Robert Huddleston. Yet, all this said and accepted, how much superior to his brothers, the educated, the well-schooled men, who, neither of them, could come near to the nature and condition of poetry? The land and his life on and with it, saved Thomas; cut-off from it, the timetable and the textbook insulating them, they could only thumb and fumble among rootless ideas and threadbare fancies. For to the hard times and the emigration, and the shattering of the old coherent order was added National Education, and the havoc it wrought unwittingly with its two-edged blade. Had not *Poems from College and Country* already been in print, it would have been necessary to invent that book, fairly to illustrate the sad end of 'an auld sang'.

The
ANTHOLOGY

INTRODUCTION
to the
ANTHOLOGY

In placing these verses before readers unfamiliar with them, I am not offering a group of masterpieces for their consideration. This selection has not been made primarily according to rigorous literary standards. Nevertheless I should remark that, earlier this year, Samuel Thomson's 'To a Hedgehog' appeared in *The Faber Book of Irish Verse* edited by John Montague, and that both 'The Weaver's Triumph' by Edward L. Sloan and 'A Song for February' by Thomas Given are in *Scottish Verse 1851–1951* chosen by Professor Douglas Young (1952). Almost a century ago, in 1879, Charles A. Read, in the second volume of his monumental repository, *The Cabinet of Irish Literature*, reprinted James Orr's 'The Irish Cottier's Death and Burial', omitting one of the stanzas which is also among those that I have left out.

The first stanza of James Campbell's 'The Devotion' and six stanzas of John McKinley's 'Winter Night in the North of Ireland' were in *Rann* No. 1, summer 1948. Thomson's 'To a Hedgehog', his 'April', James Orr's 'Winter' and Hugh Porter's 'The Muse Dismissed' appeared in *Rann* No. 11, winter 1950–1951. I there gave these in the Modern Lallans orthography.

In the present book I have not attempted to regularise the spelling in that manner, though the lack of consistency in rendering the varieties of vernacular, and what may have been the bard's own errors or the slips of the sorely-vexed printers of these erratic texts have left their evidence in the old pages. I have tampered with the words as little as possible, only here and there inserting a missing vowel, substituting a capital letter for one of lower case or striking out an awkward plural; for the shape, arrangement and condition of the words is a significant element in the quiddity of these verses. I have nevertheless given very few without cuts, for our old authors were more prolix than we now find appropriate, and I believe there is more nourishing grain in these half-loaves than in those I have left aside.

The verses illustrate the principal metrical patterns used, Standard Habbie, that neat hold-all, *The Holy Fair* stanza, *The Cherrie and the Slae* quatorzain, the eighteenth century heroic couplet with its residual poetic diction which acted as a sturdy raft to many who would, without its even planks, have sunk out of sight, the ubiquitous octosyllabic couplet, a device perilously charged with its own self-generated momentum, the anapaestic beat of many lyrics, the assonances and approximate rhymes of the dense vernacular.

These verses have also some significance in the light which they throw upon rural life in the eastern part of Ulster in the period 1800–1900.

Many of the predominant interests of the bards and their little communities are demonstrated: folk-customs and superstitions, domestic and class relationships, manual crafts, the weather and the seasons, objects seen and social practices observed, the decline of the spinning-wheel and the hand-loom, Tenant Right, education; we have here some humour, some concern for the ways of words, abundant humanity, a quick eye for deceit, an enthusiasm for physical pleasure, sentiment, love, but little or no highly creative imagination. There is no Robert Burns or John Clare to be discovered here, but the reader will encounter several companionable men and a number of memorable lines of verse.

SONNET TO A PRIMROSE

Sweet, modest flow'ret, that, beneath the thorn,
    Unfold'st thy beauties in the lonely dell,
I meet thy fragrance in the breeze of morn,
    In wilds where solitude and silence dwell.
Tho' garden flow'rs a richer tint display,
    They oft demand the planter's nicest care;
While thou appear'st beneath some shelt'ring spray,
    'Mid April's lingering frosts, and piercing air.
How like the rustic poet's lot is thine!
    Whom nature taught the simple song to raise,
Doom'd in oblivion's darkest shades to pine,
    He chaunts . . . but seldom gains the meed of
        praise
So, in some pathless desert thou art thrown,
    To shed thy sweet perfume, and fade unknown.

ANDREW McKENZIE (1780–1839)

Source: *Poems and Songs on Different Subjects*
Belfast, 1810

from THE BARD

Then at the summer's sweet return,
Low by the brink o' some bit burn,
   Or on some grassy brae,
Reclin'd he lies, wi' up-turn'd ear,
And een half steek'd, intent to hear
   The lark's melodious lay;
In this delirium, deep and ween,
   Full monie a day he spen's,
Till gray-ey'd glomin' shut the scene
   Upon him, ere he kens;
     His heart then, will start when
      He hears the wakerife rail;
     Devotion's emotions,
      O'er all his pow'rs prevail'.

Then he can sit nae longer still,
But up he gets, an' roun' the hill
   He steps sedately slow,
Straight to the weel-kent creek he hies,
While trains of bright ideas rise
   With many a grateful glow,
There prostrate falls – but O! what tongue,
   What language could declare,
What Cowper, Milton, or what Young,
   Could paint his powerful prayer?
     Then peaceful, an' graceful,
      Frae 'mang the blossom'd broom,
     He danders, an' wanders
      Towards his little home.

HUGH PORTER (1781–?)

Source: *Poetical Attempts, by Hugh Porter,
a County of Down weaver*, Belfast, 1813

HOSPITALITY

*from The Next Morning after having dined
with the Rev. Messrs. T. and B.*

Yestreen, sedate I sat beside
My T****, my frien', my country's pride,
An' him wha cross'd the ocean wide,
    An' brought us owre fu' cantie,
Upon a smooth castalian tide,
    Th' Italic *Homer, Dante.*

Yestreen, like some great night or squire,
I loll'd upon a cushion'd chair,
An' fed on rich an' dainty fare,
    Whar kindness ay comes gratis;
This morn, I on a stool maun share
    A breakfast o' potatoes.

Yestreen the privilege was mine
To drink the rich an' rosy wine
Like ony favourite o' the nine,
    And what's a serious matter,
This morn, the produce o' the vine
    Is turn'd, wi' me, to water.

HUGH PORTER

Source: op. cit.

THE MUSE DISMISSED

Be hush'd my Muse, ye ken the morn
Begins the shearing o' the corn,
Whar knuckles monie a risk maun run,
An' monie a trophy's lost an' won,
Whar sturdy boys, wi' might an' main
Shall camp, till wrists an' thumbs they strain,
While pithless, pantin' wi' the heat,
They bathe their weazen'd pelts in sweat
To gain a sprig o' fading fame,
Before they taste the dear-bought cream –
But bide ye there, my pens an' papers,
For I maun up, an' to my scrapers –
Yet, min' my lass – ye maun return
The very night we cut the Churn.

HUGH PORTER

Source: op. cit.

from THE COAL HOLE,
A STRANGE TALE

Frae Newtownards three miles or four,
Near to Mount Stewart on the sea-shore,
A man does wi' his auger bore,
    An ither tools,
Five hunner feet perhaps an' more,
    In search o' coals.

In Mexico or rich Peru,
Whare they find gold and silver too,
There's nae sic slavish wark to do,

In raisin' ore,
Nae beds o' freestane to pierce through
   Nor holes to bore.

But here, far distant frae the line,
We hae nae gowd or siller fine,
Our metal's o' a coarser kind,
   Baith lead and coal,
While copper, brass, or iron fine,
   Lies near the pole.

While one mounts in an air balloon,
To reconnoitre every town,
Ithers survey the county Down,
   To map the roads;
This man does drive his auger down,
   To the Antipodes.

But will this miner never stap,
Nor winter mak' him shut his trap,
Nor haul the tackle frae the tap,
   O' the tall trees,
Till down his tools go wi' a slap,
   I' the South Seas?

Let every matron wish guid speed,
That boils a pot, or harns her bread,
Or hings the kettle owre a gleed,
   At close o' day,
For to distill her Indian weed,
   Or brew her tea.

FRANCIS BOYLE (*c.*1730–?)

Source: *Miscellaneous Poems*, Belfast, 1811

from THE NYMPH OF THE LAGAN

Her looks are mild, her smiles are gay,
Her breath as sweet as summer weather;
　Her lovely eyes outshine the day,
The moon or stars, or both together.
　Young men lie sighing for her sake,
She's my delight and all men's wonder;
　Certainly my heart will break
If we are still to be asunder.

FRANCIS BOYLE

Source: op. cit.

THE COBBLER
from DODDERY WILLOWAIN

The night mair frightsom' aye do blow,
Whan Luna she forgets tae show;
Whan stars disdain tae show their form,
By reason o' th' approachin' storm;
Whan ower the traveller piles the heap,
O' smoorin' snaw, or splashy sleet;
Whan duck an' goose do ower us squagh,
Tae seek a shelterin' ford or loch;
Whan Christian folk hing ower th' ingle,
Harkenin' tae the bitter trimmel
O' doors weel steek'd again the win'
That's whis'lin' through the keyhole in.

On sic like night as we narrate,
Brave Doddery strowlin' ta'en the gate,
Despisin' a' that blew, no'ght fearin',
Unto a cobbler's shap careerin'.
The cobbler nae less fam'd for drolls,
Than for substantial sheetin' soles.

Now to the tale, and on we start,
The cobbler soon was at the wark
The aul' shoon quickly aff were toss'd;
Quick they were clean'd and on the last;
And on the knee were firmly placed,
An' ticht the stirrup ower them laced:
Wi' every clink the aul' hook's dirl,
A' roun' like shot the tacks did birl –
The ancient knife now raspin' sharps,
An' through the ox hide wheezelin' starts;
And now the elson eddyin' bores,
The weel wax'd en' now whizzin' snores;
While sturdy 'rist wi' tradesman's sough,
Weel nedds't thegether wi' a pegh.

ROBERT HUDDLESTON

Source: *A Collection of Poems and Songs on Rural Subjects*,
Belfast, 1844

from THE LAMMAS FAIR
(BELFAST)

In twa's an' three's right on they flock,
    The morn's gat up an' clearsom',
An' a' the course ae w'y direct:
    An' now in droves, see here's some
Wi' bleered e'e, an' dirty face,
    Wha couldna sleep to think o't;
Wha's travell'd ten lang miles or this,
    An' had a noble rant o't
            Sae air this day.

On right they drive, some 'thout their shoes,
    And some in jirgin' leather;
Some aul' folks their smoakin' gaes,
    The slever times the bleather.
Here gangs a wife sae laden'd doon,
    Wi' mony a creashy treasure;
Wha scarce can thraw her neck ha'f roun,
    Tae bid guid morn her neighbour,
            As pass'd that day.

Yeir basket Kates are skelpin' on,
    An' passin' a' they're seein';
Their petticoats weel kilt ahin,
    Nor dub or stoure mismay 'em.
An' ho! my grannie snugly slips
    Tae mak' her ainie market,
Wi' mantle neat, and dowdy cap,
    Made o' a weel bleech'd sark it,
            Fu' douce that day.

In clackin' tugs are naigies yock't –
    They're hippin' and they're hoyin';
The bleatin' lambs are gaun in flocks –
    They're scuddin' loofs an' buyin':
There, asses bound between their creels,
    Fill'd fu' o' bra' big herrin';
Here, ither beece wi' prataes, meals,
    Frae a' parts o' aul' Erin,
        For sale that day.

The worse o' wear here spavied yads,
    Wi' weel brush'd hair ower bruises;
On wham the smith haes spent on shods,
    A week tae fit their hovies.
Wi' ancient snouts nigh tae the grin.
    They're dreamin' as they travel;
Wi' boots an' spurs their whipper-in,
    Yet scarce can mak' them kevel,
        Frae sleep that day.

Awow! an' got in Poultry Square,
    How mony lasses smilin';
An' see them wi' their butter ware,
    An' eggs an' fowl beguilin'.
But Rantana the bellman comes,
    The constable's amang them;
And ha! he's libbin' yon aul' rung,
    An' for her doonright rangin'
        For fun that day.

Ding-dong, again haes rung the bell,
    Corn factors don't hae't gratis! –
And Lord preserve yon man does sell
    The poor man's food, the pretaes,

:

Ance mair ding-dong; 'hurrah' the cry,
    Here asses, an' here truckles;
'Girls what ye like again come buy' –
    By gobs! see you'er cockles,
            For sale that day.

Yon birky lo! behold! him dress'd,
    Some sprigtail frae the clarkin';
Wi' cut an' capor see how sprush'd,
    Sae bra' new out he's startin'.
He's thruppens left yet for the shine,
    Wi' velvet collar glitterin';
Och! girls beware, he'll tak' ye in,
    A gentleman's the slautern
            Sae trim this day.

In Smithfield as I toddled through,
    The dread uproar was deavin';
Wi' tinsel'd frock, an' painted brow,
    The pappit show seemed lievin'.
A bulk o' fo'k aroun' was clad,
    O' a' kin's you could mention;
Tae see aul' Jerry wi' the wig,
    An' miter'd frocks a' dancin',
            For pense that day.

Wi' tassel'd caps an' gleamin' blades,
    Wi' fifein' an' wi' drummin';
The red coat boys now on parade,
    They shake the grun they're gaun on:
An' clout the sheepskin yet extends,
    An' wheeper's louder blawin';
Till after them fu' mony wend,
    An' some's up tae them jawin'
            Right glib that day.

The music quats – the serjeant cries,
   Big bounty don't resist it;
A jug o' punch boys, don't despise,
   A soger's life's the best o't.
An' see how many blackguard rogues,
   An' strappin' billies listenin';
Wi' courage bauld charm'd ower their sads,
   An' cagy shillin's fistin',
         Wha'll rue't some day.

There sits a tinker wi' his tins,
   A turner wi' his ladles;
A gleg tongu'd spunkie's cryin' spoons,
   Anither's at her fables.
Billowre! a singer's come tae han',
   The crowd is geather'd roun' her;
A pick-pocket them slips amang,
   His booty there to plun'er
         Wi' craft that day.

Yeir Chaeny-mem is dinglin' loud,
   Her bonnie cup an' saucer;
But presently there tak's her lug,
   A fist that is a fasher.
'Wad ye sell a' the day yeirsel',
   An' no gie me a share o't?'
Whan turns about aul' fisty Nell,
   The offender's ower wi' bare hip,
         Clean felt that day.

On this side sits a ging'-bread Joe,
   The tither a grozet barrow;
The plumbs are here – ilk black's a sloe,
   Melts in yeir mouth like marrow.

This way sit barley-sugar Jones,
    Across there apple factors;
The cutler wi' his wheel an' hone's,
    Beside the man an' pictures;
        At wark that day.

Here's yellow-man, an' tuffy sweet,
    Girls will ye taste or pree it;
An aul' wife crys gaun through the street,
    'Boys treat yeir sweethearts tae it.'
'Och, here's the better stuff for them,
    Teetotal sure's the cordial' –
Na, na, quo' Frank, a glass o' rum
    'Fore soda water's preferable
        On onnie day.

Yeir pedlar catches mak' their crum's,
    The shamy duds they're playin';
Some sair niest morn they'll eat their thum's,
    For what th' day they're payin'.
Yon fellow's buyin' twa gash cames,
    For his wee Jenny's fairin';
Anither's at the gilt brass rings –
    They're gowd the pimp's declarin',
        Tae him that day.

The fo'k are gaun on every side,
    I'm gaun tae see what ails them;
So, follow'd on ahint the crowd,
    Till I arriv'd at raildom.
As luckin' a' for somethin' strange,
    On tiptoe a' they're sprawlin';
As if some ane wi' lousy mange,
    Was a' out ower crawlin',
        They stare that day.

Halloo! ahead there comes a shout —
　　'Come, clear the w'y, be hasty;
Soon, soon, ye'll see a flysome brute,
　　Wi' fire that wad roast ye.'
But forth it comes a rowtin' ill,
　　Fleet as the win' careerin';
'Soho! avaunt! keep clear the rail,'
　　The 'deil ma care' wha's fearin'
　　　　It cam' that day.

While now confusion crowns the noise,
　　An' expectation's waiter;
While presently a' 's in surprise,
　　The reek attracts an' vapour.
I'm stoitin' through like onnie stoge,
　　Amang yeir great big nobles;
Remarkin' no'ght as being odd,
　　Tho' a' astonish'd govels
　　　　Tae see't that day.

Ohone! 'tis aul' Nick chain'd on wheels,
　　Wi' reekin' fiery furnace;
Wha's targin' on a train o' hells,
　　Back, forret tae Lisburnes.
An' how now Michael can ye la'gh,
　　At king o' a' the witches —
A wee bit in, again it's aff,
　　This time before't the coaches,
　　　　Like mad that day.

ROBERT HUDDLESTON

Source: op. cit.

from CREEVY HALL

The eve got dusk, the wind was still,
   The Corncraik turned her haverl lyre,
And far away o'er Seefar-Hill,
   The Cuckoo's chorus joined the choir;
The thrush sang drowsy day to rest,
   In Anderson's lone sylvan shaw;
And onward, as I homeward pressed,
   The Redbreast sung by Creevy Ha'.

ROBERT HUDDLESTON

Source: *A Collection of Poems and Songs*, Vol. 2,
Belfast, 1846

from THE WEAVER'S TRIUMPH

It was but yestreen I had oot my bit claith, man,
   Tuk it under my arm, doun tae Balford I went,
Untae the Braid Square, tae wee cockit Rab's
     warehoose –
   For a trifle o' cash, man, it was my intent.
My noddle bein' reeming wi' stoups o' guid liquor,
   I marched in fu' stately and throwed the dud
     down,
Whan a cock-o'-the-north o' a foreman, ca'd
     Hudson,
   Whispered tae his employer – 'We'll gi'e him a
     croon.'

My wee bit o' labour bein' thrown on the counter,
   Wi' butterfly's een tae examine't he goes;
He hemmed and he ha'd, and he swore it was
     shameless,

Syne oot wi' his snoot-cloot and dighted his nose.
He swore that the warp would been better by
    double –
  For their penny collars 'twas nae use ava;
Though the price o' my labour was just half-a-
    guinea,
  He would gi'e me a shilling and let me awa.

I glowered at the ape wi' twa een like red cinders,
  While wee cockit Rab at his knavery did wink;
Quo' I, 'Honest foreman, ye ha'e turned a barber,
  Tae shave simple weavers sae neatly, I think;
But haud ye, a jiffey, my potstick-legged callan –
  For my nine-and-sixpence I'll gi'e ye some fun:
I'll ca' doun your betters tae think on your capers,
  And see if you'll rob me, you half-stocked gun.'

Noo, twa honest neebours together convened,
  And examined it weel, frae beginning tae end;
And the verdict they gi'en was, 'Return him his
    money,
  Or before Parson Wilkins you'll ha'e tae attend.'
My money I pouched wi' a rollickin' smirk –
O Oh! what was the look that his foremanship
    gi'en!
Quo' I, 'Honest foreman, act somewhat mair justly:
  You see arbitration's but seldom your frien'.'

EDWARD L. SLOAN

Source: *The Bard's Offering: A Collection of Miscellaneous Poems*,
Belfast, 1854

MAY EVE
from The Year's Holidays

Time flies – 'tis April's latest day,
Eve to the first-born morn in May,
And youths use superstition's arts
To know the conq'rors of their hearts.
The simple yarrow leaves its bed,
Lies placed with care beneath the head,
To charm bright fancy's love-lit dream,
And give of future life a gleam;
The harmless, unoffensive snail,
Confined, must mark, with slimy trail,
The initials of the only name
Which lights that bosom with a flame.

EDWARD L. SLOAN

Source: op. cit.

HALLOWEEN
from The Year's Holidays

Now pass we August's roseate hues –
Its sunsets, rich with burnished views;
September's fields of whitened grain,
The toil-worn labourer's pride and gain;
October, with its lesson stern,
Which young and old alike may learn,
That, as the falling leaves descend,
Man sees the shadow of his end,
And gladly welcoming, perceive,
Approaching far-famed Hallow-eve.

'Tis night, and loudly does the noise
Arise from mischief-making boys,
Who meet prepared for 'raising fun,'
And start forth at a rapid run –
Knock loudly at each door, and fly,
Ere scarce the inmates know they're nigh.

Within, primeval mirth abounds,
And jokes prevail, and laughter sounds.
The welcome apples soon appear;
The good-man draws the table near,
And equally 'gins to divide
The fruit the matron's care supplied.

A tub the youngsters quick procure,
And place, with water, on the floor:
Some little elves the apples drop,
Which lightly float upon the top;
Now, head and shoulders bare, each tries,
With open mouth, to seize the prize;
Some sudden dash, and miss their aim;
Some slowly follow round the game,
Drive to the bottom, that they may,
In dripping triumph, win the play.

EDWARD L. SLOAN

Source: op. cit.

from THE CHURN

A boone attacks a golden field
    In bright September's morn;
And keen the glancing hooks they wield,
    And fast they fell the corn.
Jokes fly like lightning, while the grain
    Waves o'er their stooping heads,
And laughter, mocking toil and pain,
    Like Sunday sunshine spreads.

Up from the lough the Autumn breeze
    Through reeds and osiers sighed,
While round the field the aspen trees
    In soothing sounds replied.
High on the uplands cawed the rooks,
    The swimmers ploughed the water,
And far were seen through golden stooks
    The golden windows glitter.

'Hurroo my boys,' their leader cries,
    'Today we win the *Churn*!'
Then flashed with light their sickles bright,
    Down sweeping through the corn.
With bodies lithe, and spirits blithe,
    In spite of toil or trouble,
Each reaped his *sett* as with a scythe,
    Then rested on the stubble.

Now rich sweetmilk and buttered bread
    Were handed round the boone,
And scarce a reaper raised a head
    From that again till noon.
But still in volleys flew the fun

Through all the merry morn,
Till half the busy day was done,
    And twanged the dinner horn.

Then on again the current swept
    Of jokes and stories funny,
Till every stalk was stooked except
    The *loghter* for the *granny*.
A handful, heavy, strong, and tall,
    Bold Sam and Susy platted;
And then prepared they, one and all,
    To fling their sickles at it.

Some only haggled it below,
    And some flew o'er its crown,
Till Bridget aimed a shearing blow
    That fairly fetched it down.
Then blithely tossing from the *brace*
    The old one limp and sooty,
The new adorned the chimney place
    In all its golden beauty.

Now ranged on benches, stools and chairs,
    They fill the house with glee,
While every youngster gaily bears
    A sweetheart on his knee.
And perfect pleasure and content
    From happy faces beam,
As firstly round the ranks are sent
    The *noggins* full of cream.

HENRY McDONALD FLECHER (1827–? LIVING IN 1909)

Source: *Poems, Songs and Ballads*, Belfast, 1866

MARRIED FOR MONEY

I married for money, I married for lan',
I got what I married but missed a man;
I have lashins to live on and little to do,
A husband I loathe and a life to rue!

Oh, I was a saucy extravagant belle,
And I jilted the lad that I loved so well
For one that could keep me up idle and gay,
And now I may cry salt tears my day!

He's a meddlin', peddlin', sneevelin' elf
That niver loved sowl but his own sweet self;
A tyrant with weemen, a coward with men –
How different that from my own brave Ben?

Betther, wrapped in a rug on a bean-strow bed
By the boy of your fancy to boulster your head,
Than be curtained with silk and be nestled in
     down
Where it isn't by love but the law you're boun'.

O girls be warned by your comrade Ann,
And marry no mortal for money or lan';
What's lashins to live on and little to do
With a husband you hate and a marriage you rue?

HENRY McDONALD FLECHER

Source: op. cit.

THE EPICURE'S ADDRESS TO BACON

O Fortune! thou hast been propitious,
As I on bacon am voracious –
To worship't would be superstitious,
   Or I would try it;
For, Lord! it is the most delicious
   Soul of diet.

Thy praise, O bacon! shall be sung,
Unto new life thou hast me brung;
To see my brace wie flitches strung,
   Just in my sight;
My auld pan shall be neatly hung
   This very night.

Nae paintful gripes, nor gut contraction,
I need nae doctor's sly inspection,
Or trouble them for an injection,
   To purge or thin me;
'Tis easy seen, by my complexion,
   The juice is in me.

My tripes they are completely swampit,
Nae aches nor pains my joints since crampit,
Wi' fervour I cry, Lord be thankit,
   Each day I dine;
I revere the power on matter stampit
   The form of swine.

To tell my state I'll now propose,
The pearly drops roll down my nose,
I yawn, and grinders there disclose
   A pig could tear;

I yawn again, then up them close,
  And say nae mair.

Nae animal in all creation
Deserves so much my approbation,
It keeps my tripes in a right station,
  Without crack or chasm;
'Tis of mair use to my salvation
  Than holy chrism.

Though Dives, that renowned glutton,
Was damned for eating beef and mutton,
Wi' ither trash he put his gut in,
  And drinking wine;
There's nane yet damned, I'll lay a button,
  For eating swine.

Moses and Aaron, the auld priest,
Forbade the folk to eat this beast,
They might as well hae held their whist –
  I'd think nae evil,
Could I but get my guts weel creesht,
  To eat the Devil.

I lang hae strove, some thought in vain,
To get a pig just of my ain;
That blissful summit I did gain,
  And am begun
To gormandize, my guts I'll strain
  Out like a tun.

I like swine's grease, some think it odd,
I scarce prefer the grace of God;
They sell their pigs to chiels abroad,

For yellow coin;
The Devil o'er them ride rough-shod,
  Ere they get mine.

Some like their spirits up to cheer,
With good strong whiskey, or brown beer,
Some like their brains for to keep clear,
  By wine applying;
Nae music ever charmed my ear,
  Like pork a frying.

JAMES CAMPBELL (1758–1818)

Source: *The Posthumous Works of James Campbell of Ballynure*, Belfast, 1820

THE DEVOTION

On a fine dewy morning, in the sweet month of May,
My duty performing, I walked forth to pray;
Twas at that prayer-meeting this maid I did see,
And, though church was my notion, my devotion
  got she.

Her graceful deportment my attention close drew,
Till the whole congregation of my station got view;
I was seized by a stupor my senses did confound,
Till the book from my hand fell direct to the ground.

To describe my emotion, in my notion 'tis vain,
For my bosom was burning with pleasure and pain;
Life's fluids quick back on my heart did recoil,
Had I prayed in my closet, 'twould have saved all
  my toil.

Her hair a fine nut-brown, and inclining to pale,
Her skin like bleached linen, or snow on the vale;
Her voice like an organ, mild, clear, soft, and sweet,
It my notion of devotion twined on her complete.

JAMES CAMPBELL

Source: op. cit.

MOLLY HUME

Come each gay sporter or maiden courter,
Hear Alex. Porter his love declare,
Of a farmer's daugther near Six-mile-water,
Whose hopes did flatter his love sincere;
But now she's left me, of joy bereft me.
She has distressed me and sealed my doom;
My heart is wounded with grief unbounded,
My senses drowned by Molly Hume.

Though she was deceiving for her I am grieving,
And when I am weaving I oft times say,
Though my time I wasted, some love I tasted,
When locked within her sweet arms I lay.
But now she is wedded and also bedded,
Another young man enjoys my room;
This female enchanter, though I must want her,
My love shall still haunt her – fy, Molly Hume.

JAMES CAMPBELL

Source: *The Poems and Songs of James Campbell of Ballynure with additional songs not before published*, Ballyclare, 1870

from TO A HEDGEHOG

Thou grimmest far o' gruesome tykes
Grubbing thy food by thorny dykes,
Gudefaith thou disna want for pikes
   Baith sharp an' rauckle;
Thou looks (Lord save's) array'd in spikes,
   A creepin' heckle . . .

Sure Nick begat thee, at the first,
On some auld whin or thorn accurst;
An' some horn-fingered harpie nurst
   The ugly urchin:
Then Belzie, laughin' like to burst
   First ca'd thee *Hurchin*.

Folk tell how thou, sae far frae daft,
When wind-fa'n fruit lie scatter'd saft,
Will row thysel' wi' cunning craft,
   An' bear awa'
Upon thy back, what fares thee aft
   A day or twa.

But whether this account be true
Is mair than I will here avow;
If that thou stribs the outler cow,
   As some assert,
A pretty milkmaid, I allow
   Forsooth though art . . .

Now creep awa the way ye came
And tend your squeakin' pups at hame;
Gin Colley should o'erhear the same,
   It might be fatal

For you, wi' a' the pikes ye claim
  Wi' him to battle.

SAMUEL THOMSON (1766–1816)

Source: *New Poems*, Belfast, 1799

APRIL

Behold the ever-tim'rous hare,
Already quits her furzy shade,
And o'er the field, with watchful care,
Unseen to nip the sprouting blade.

Adown the whin-beskirted way
Thoughtless plods the schoolboy young,
At times in haste – anon he'll stay
And thinks he hears the cuckoo's song.

SAMUEL THOMSON

Source: op. cit.

THE COTTIER'S BED

Behold the bed of simple Sawney's rest,
With cobwebs trimm'd, in many a mazy coil,
Where, in a wifie's fond embraces blest
The sturdy clown forgets his daily toil.
Here, lock'd in sleep, which no wild dreams
    infest,
Amid his offspring, lies the brawny sire;

While balmy Health, on every cheek imprest,
Blooms like the blossom on the wild wood brier,
And when awaken'd by his chanticleer,
That loud and fearless from the hallan crows,
The churl array's him in his ragged gear
And whistling chearful, to his labour goes.
Unknown, unknowing, thus from year to year.
His useful life in even tenour flows.

SAMUEL THOMSON

Source: op. cit.

from TO THE POTATOE

I ledge we'd fen gif fairly quat o'
The weed we smoke, an' chow the fat o';
An' wadna grudge to want the wat o'
    Wealth-wastin' Tea;
But leeze me on the precious Pratoe,
    My country's stay!

Bright blooms the Bean that scents the valley,
An' bright the Pea, that speels the salie,
An' bright the Plumb tree, blossom't brawly,
    An' blue-bow't lint;
But what wi' straught rais't raws can tally,
    That sun-beams tint.

Waeworth the proud prelatic pack,
Wha Point an' Prataoes downa tak!
With *them* galore, an' whyles a plack
    To mak' me frisky,

I'll fen, an' barley freely lack –
  Except in whisky.

Sweet in the mornin', after dashlin',
Thy daigh is, pouther't owre wi' mashlin;
Creesh't scons stan' pil't on plates, or brislin'
  A' roun' the ingle,
While a fand *Wifie* fast is fislin,
  An tea-cups jingle.

Sweet to the boons that blythely enter
At dinner-time, the graise in centre,
Champ't up wi' kail, that pey the planter,
  Beans, pa'snips, peas!
Gosh! cud a cautious Covenanter
  Wait for the grace?

JAMES ORR (1770–1816)

Source: *Poems on Various Subjects*, Belfast, 1804

WRITTEN IN WINTER

The green warl's awa, but the white ane can charm
    them
  Wha skait on the burn, or wi' settin' dogs rin:
The hind's dinlin' han's, numb't we snaw-baws, to
    warm them,
  He claps on his hard sides, whase doublets are thin.

How dark the hail show'r mak's yon vale, aince sae
    pleasin'!

How laigh stoops the bush that's owre-burden't wi'
   drift!
The icicles dreep at the half-thow't house-easin',
   Whan blunt the sun beams frae the verge o' the lift.

The hedge-hauntin' blackbird, on ae fit whyles restin',
   Wad fain heat the tither in storm-rufflet wing;
The silly sweel't sheep, ay the stifflin' storm breastin',
   Are glad o' green piles at the side o' the spring.

JAMES ORR

Source: op. cit.

THE WANDERER

'Wha's there?' she ax't. The wan'rers rap
   Against the pane the lassie scaur'd:
The blast that bray'd on *Slimiss* tap
   Wad hardly let a haet be heard.
'A frien',' he cried, 'for common crimes
   Tost thro' the country fore and aft' –
'Mair lown,' quo' she – thir's woefu' times! –
   'The herd's aboon me on the laft.'

'I call'd,' he whisper'd, 'wi' a wight
   Wham aft I've help'd wi' han' an' purse;
He wadna let me stay a' night –
   Weel! sic a heart's a greater curse:
But Leezie's gentler. Hark that hail!
   This piercin' night is rougher far' –
'Come roun',' she said, 'an' shun the gale,
   I'm gaun to slip aside the bar.'

'Waes me! how wat ye're? Gie's your hat,
    An' dry your face wi' something – hae.
In sic a takin', weel I wat;
    I wad preserve my greatest fae:
We'll mak' nae fire; the *picquet* bauld
    Might see the light, an' may be stap;
But I'll sit up: my bed's no cauld,
    Gae till't awee an' tak' a nap.'

JAMES ORR

Source: op. cit.

THE IRISH COTTIER'S
DEATH AND BURIAL

Wi' patient watchfu'ness, lasses an' lads,
    Carefu' an' kin', surroun' his clean caff bed,
Ane to his lips the coolin' cordial ha'ds,
    An' ane behin' supports his achin' head;
    Some bin' the arm that lately has been bled,
An' some burn bricks his feet mair warm to mak;
    If e'er he doze, how noiselessly they tread!
An' stap the lights to mak the bield be black,
An' aft the bedside lea, an' aft slip saftly back.

Rang'd roun' the hearth, where he presides nae mair,
    Th' inquirin' nybers mourn their sufferin' frien';
An' now an' then divert awa their care,
    By tellin' tales to please some glaiket wean,
    Wha's e'e soon fills whan told about the pain
Its sire endures, an' what his loss wad be;
    An' much they say, but a', alas! in vain,

To soothe the mither, wha ha'f pleas'd could see
Her partner eas'd by death, though for his life she'd die.

And while they're provin' that his end is sure
   By strange ill omens – to assuage his smart
The minister comes in, wha' to the poor,
     Without a fee performs the doctor's part:
     An' while wi' hope he soothes the suff'rer's heart,
An' gies a cheap, safe recipe, they try
   To quat braid Scotch, a task that foils their art;
For while they join his converse, vain though shy,
They monie a lang learn'd word misca' an' misapply.

Belyve an auld man lifts the Word o' God,
   Gies out a line, an' sings o' grief an' pain;
Reads o'er a chapter, chosen as it should,
     That maks them sure the dead shall rise again;
     An' prays, that he, wha's hand has gie'n and ta'en,
May be the orphan's guide, the widow's stay;
   An' that, rememb'rin' death ere health be gane,
They a' may walk in wisdom's Heaven-ward way,
Like him, the man o' worth, that's now a clod o' clay.

Cou'd he whose limbs they decently hae stretch'd,
   The followers o' freets awake an' mark,
What wad he think o' them, he oft beseeched
     To be mair wise than mind sic notions dark?
     To bare the shelves o' plates they fa' to wark;
Before the looking-glass a claith they cast;
   An' if a clock were here, nae ear might hark
Her still'd han's tell how hours an' moments pass'd;
Ignorance bred sic pranks, an' custom gars them last.

But see what crowds to wauk the Cottier come!
  Maist frae respect, but some to gape-seed saw:
Douce men an' wives step forward to the room,
  The youths on forms sit rang'd roun' like wa';
  Some at a plate light pipes as white as snaw;
Some hark in neuks wi' lasses whom they prize;
  Some banter simple nymphs, their parts to shaw;
But though a laugh be sometimes like to rise,
They dinna either death or the deceas'd despise.

An' now a striplin', wi' becomin grace,
  Han's the wauk-supper, in a riddle, roun';
Hard bread, an' cheese, might nicest palates please,
  Bought frae a huxter in the nyb'rin' town;
  An' gi'es them gills a piece o' rum sae brown,
By polished sots wi' feign'd reluctance pried;
  Though here an' there may sit a menseless loun,
The thoughtfu' class consider poor folks need,
An' only 'kiss the cup,' an' hardly ance break bread.

Syne wi' anither glass they hail day-light,
  An' crack mair cruse o' bargains, farms, an' beasts;
Or han' tradition down, an' ither fright,
  Wi' dreadfu' tales o' witches, elves, an' ghaists.
  The soger lad, wha on his pension rests,
Tells how he fought, an' proudly bares his scaur;
  While unfledg'd gulls, just looking owre their nests,
Brag how they lately did their rivals daur,
Before their first sweethears, an' dashed them i' the
      glaur.

An' while some lass, though on their cracks intent,
  Turns to the light and sleely seems to read,
The village sires, wha kent him lang, lament

The dear deceas'd, an' praise his life an' creed;
  For if they crav'd his help in time o' need,
Or gied him trust, they prov'd him true an' kin';
  'But he,' they cry, 'wha blames his word or deed,
Might say the sun, that now begins to shine,
Is rising i' the wast, whare he'll at e'en decline.'

Warn'd to the Cottier's burial, rich an' poor
  Cam' at the hour, tho' win' an' rain beat sair;
An' monie met it at the distant moor,
    An' duly, time-about, bore up the bier,
    That four men shouther'd through the church-yard
      drear.
Twa youths knelt down, and humbly in the grave
  Laid their blest father. Numbers shed a tear,
Hop'd for an end like his, and saftly strave
To calm his female frien's, wha dolefully did rave.

An' while the sexton earth'd his poor remains,
  The circling crowd contemplatively stood,
An' mark'd the empty sculls, an' jointless banes,
    That, cast at random, lay like cloven wood:
    Some stept outbye, an' read the gravestanes rude,
That only tald the inmates' years an' names;
    An' ithers, kneeling, stream'd a saut, saut flood,
On the dear dust that held their kinsfolks' frames –
Then, through the gate they a' pass'd to their diff'rent
      hames.

JAMES ORR

Source: *The Posthumous Works of James Orr, of Ballycarry,
with a Sketch of his Life*, Belfast, 1817

BE THIS MY LOT

A cow and a pig, and a bonny bit land,
A trifle of money still at my command,
To live independent, – I love to be free,
A competent portion is plenty for me.

I never will scramble to heap up a store,
For heir's wide to scatter when I am no more;
Nor yet will I squander what heaven has lent,
But plenish my cabin, and pay up the rent.

And when I'm a husband, may I have a wife
Who'll make it her study to sweeten my life,
And love to be thrifty, and careful of all,
That things may be decent when visitors call.

JOHN DICKEY

Source: *Poems on Various Subjects,* Belfast, 1818

from ADDRESS TO PARKGATE

Now o'er the Craigs where furze so prickly grew,
The hand of Ceres spreads the harvest hue,
And shady groves now cover the old *rais*
Where in the sun we basked in summer days,
And, from the foot of each old mossy stone,
Pulled the blae-berries gladly one by one.
Now coos the woodquest in the rising grove
Where I have often with the warping drove
Of Shinny Players, ended many a hail
Or buttons pitched, and then tossed head or tail.

Blest days! when I the noisy mansion sought
Where Hefferen long thy clam'rous school has taught
To cypher well, or deeply to explore
The rules of English, Greek or Latin lore,
Full many a night and morning have I strayed
From hedge to hedge, or thro' the fragrant shade,
My task neglecting, anxiously in quest
Of wild Bee's hive, or Yellowhammer's nest.
Forgetting all the terrors that await,
To mark the blockhead's or the truant's fate.

JOHN DICKEY

Source: op. cit.

TO A REDBREAST

*Who flew in at the author's window one
morning, during a heavy fall of snow.*

O, Robin, but you're sair forlorn!
Your plumes wi' winter war are torn;
The warld's white wi' snaw this morn,
    And yet drift's thick; –
I hae a pickle groats o' corn,
    For you to pick.

Let na mishap your spirits daunt; –
I've been mysel aft times in want;
But yet my cot the needy haunt,
    Tho' unco bare;
And let my meal be e'er sae scant,
    I gie a share.
And Robin, I'll provide for thee

Till spring wi' blossoms dress the tree,
And ope the floweret on the lee; –
Then let you gang
Back to the grove, whare bonnilie
Ye'll sing your sang.

JOHN McKINLEY

Source: *Poetic Sketches descriptive of The Giant's Causeway
and the Surrounding Scenery: with some Detached Pieces,
by John McKinley, Dunseveric*, Belfast, 1819

EAGLE AT FAIR HEAD

Now rous'd from grey Benmore's stupendous height,
The soaring eagle wings his rapid flight:
Through the expanse of Heaven behold him fly –
The sullen pirate of the rock and sky.
Around his beak what radiant glories gleam! –
His piercing eye-balls brave the solar beam:
Till near the heath-clad ridges of Knocklaid,
Swift as a shaft of light from Heaven displayed,
Prone down he darts to rob the harmless dam,
And from her bosom rends her tender lamb;
Or, fiercely pouncing on the timid hare,
He mounts again the boundless realms of air,
Wheels to his eyrie's cloudy altitude,
And tears the prey to feed his callow brood.

JOHN McKINLEY

Source: op. cit.

A WINTER NIGHT IN THE
NORTH OF IRELAND

When surly winter 'gins to blaw,
An robe himself wi' frost and snaw;
See roun' the ingle, in a raw,
   The rural folks
Sit down and pass the time awa,
   In cracks and jokes.

The grey haired couple cozey sit,
Weel pleased to hear the youngsters' wit;
The guidman maks and coals the split,
   And mends the fire,
And snuffs and smokes as he thinks fit,
   Like ony squire.

The bleezin fire o' sod and peet,
Gars some sit back, and ithers sweat,
And thaws the amaist frozen feet
   O' rustic Will,
Wha' scoured the muirs, through snaw and sleet,
   His e'e to fill.

The winsome matron at the wheel,
Wi' canny e'e keeks at the chiel
She thinks wad fit her Jenny weel;
   An sighs to see
Her careless smile, her heart o' steel,
   And scornfu' e'e.

The waefu' cause she needna spier,
Why Will, wi' a' his weel got gear,
Meets nae return but aye a sneer,

Frae foolish Jean,
For she remembers wi' a tear,
　　Wha comes between.

Their cotter's son, a canny blade,
Right skilfu' in the wooin trade,
Set a' his gins, and gript the maid
　　Fair by the heart;
Nor frae him could they keep the jade,
　　Wi' a' their art.

The rustic smokes, and talks o' lear,
Or how folk may mak muckle mair,
By risin early, takin care,
　　An spendin nane;
Nor fails to please the runkled pair,
　　Into the bane.

They talk o' houses, lan' and kye,
When this ane calves, an that ane's dry,
And how folk's hurried, that maun buy
　　Baith milk an' butter;
For plash o' tea, it's waur than whye, –
　　It's but het water.

Neist tales o' ghaists and magic spell –
O' witches lowin out o' hell,
And tricks o' Nickie-ben himsel',
　　Gae roun and roun,
Till ilka youngster thinks, pell mell
　　He's comin down.

But time, that flies though we sit still,
Brings roun' the hour, that sorry Will

Maun cross the eerie glen, or rill
  O' murmurin lay:
The auld son puts him owre the hill,
  And points the way.

JOHN McKINLEY

Source: op. cit.

COLLECTING SEABIRDS' EGGS

Where bold Kinramer's chalky steep
Stands rugged o'er the raging deep,
Like spider down his flimsy thread,
The danger great, though small the dread,
Depending all on aid divine,
And brawny strength, and hempen twine,
Down glides the kerne o'er rifted crags,
To rob the brine-bird of her eggs,
Ransacks each crevice, gains his prey,
The brittle booty bears away;
Triumphant up the dizzy road,
Exulting proudly with his load,
Wends to his crib with careless toil,
And there displays the shelly spoil;
When all his tiny younkers throng,
With tongues loquacious, loud, and long,
As round the creaking creel they fly,
How wildly rise their bursts of joy.

THOMAS BEGGS (1789–1847)

Source: *Rathlin; A descriptive poem, written after a visit to that island*, second edition, Belfast, n.d. [1844]

from THE AULD WIFE'S ADDRESS
TO HER SPINNING WHEEL

Frae Tibbie Gordon I gat this wheel,
  An' then I was young, an' my face was fair,
An' since the first day she cam' into my shiel,
  We aye had something to keep an' to spare.
On the wintry night by the clear ingle side,
  My wee bit lamp hung laigh in the lum;
An' I sung my sang, an' my wheel I plied,
  An' Rorie was pleased wi' the hartsome hum.
But now upon her I maun spin nae mair,
An' it mak's my heart baith sorry an' sair.

Now fare thee weel, my cantie wee wheel,
  In age an' youth my staff an' my stay,
How gladly at gloamin, my kind auld chiel
  Has reeled our pirn, sae bonnie an' blae
But men o' cunning an' pelf, an' pride,
  Hae made thee a useless thing to me;
For they carena what puir bodies betide,
  Or whether they live on the yirth or die.
Now the feck o' my fare is a heart fu' o' wae
An' the fourth o' a groat is the wage o' a day.

The mountain lass, at her wee bit wheel,
  How blythe was her e'e, an' how rosy her
    cheek!
Her bosom was white, an' her heart was leal, –
  Her mien it was modest, her manner was
    meek;
But now the pert maidens, wha ply in the mill,
  How wan is their visage, – how dim is their e'e
For the ban they maun bide is enough to chill

The spring o' the heart au' to deaden their
    glee:
To toil for men that are hard to please,
In a hot-bed rank wi' vice an disease.

An' when they speak, it maun be wi a squeal;
    They maun rise an' rin at the toll o' the bell,
An' brook the insult o' a tyrant an' de'il,
    An' the jargon they hear is the language o' hell.
To breed a bit lassie in sic a vile place,
    Instead o' her ain father's cot on the green,
It puts the puir thing in a pitifu case –
    Ah! black was the day when they made the
      machine.
It has added mair pelf to the hoards o' the great
And left those that were low in a far lower state.

But weel I remember langsyne, that I,
    When Rorie had little outbye to dae,
Gat aye meat enough an' some claes forbye,
    By keepin' thee busy, an' birrin' away;
An' what though we never could boast o' our
      gear
    An' what tho' we never were blest wi a bairn;
For cauld or hunger we hadna to fear,
    An' I sung my sang, an' I spun my yarn;
But nae mair for mysel' can I provide,
In these wearifu' days o' poortith an' pride.

An' when I was rade, an' hale, an' young,
    My thread cam' level, an' fine as a hair,
An' the kitten purred, an' the cricket sung,
    An the care o' my heart, was a lightsome care.
Now men ha'e erected a new ingine,

An' left but little for us to earn,
An' little for me but to pinch au' to pine;
  I wish I had died when I was a bairn, –
For my guid auld man he has breathed his last,
An' I on the cauldrife warld am cast.

THOMAS BEGGS

Source: *The Poetical Works of Thomas Beggs*, Ballyclare, n.d.
[1867]

from THE AULD WIFE'S LAMENT
FOR HER TEAPOT

Alas! alas! what shall I do,
My auld black pot is broke in two,
In which I did sae often brew
  The wee drap tea,
And thought it would ha'e cheer'd me through
  Life's weary way.

A better pot, sure, ne'er was made,
It wadna vent the sma'est blade;
Still when the tablecloth was laid
  And it appear'd
A smile out o'er my visage played,
  And a' things cheer'd.

Before I brought it frae the town
It cost me nearly half-a-crown,
Nor did I grudge't, it was sae roun',
  And very snug –
At every party it was down,
  Throughout Dunclug.

Lang after it cam' to our house
I kept it for our Sunday's use;
But when my daughters a' got spruce,
   And wanted men,
Ah! then it got the sore abuse
   Baith but and ben!

Whene'er their wooers cam' to see them,
A wee drap tea they be to gie them,
For fear, as I thought, they would lea' them,
   Alone to rove,
They never fail'd wi' sweets to free them
   Frae ithers love.

'Twas then my teapot had to thole
The power of mony a blazing coal,
Which knaw'd me to the very soul
   To hear it crackin',
While they prepar'd the butter'd roll
   For lads to smack on.

They burn'd it till it was as thin
As my auld wrinkled bluidless skin,
I still must say it was a sin
   To use it sae
For lads that didna care a pin
   About their tea.

But now my daughters a' are wed,
And health and peace frae me are fled,
I find it hard to earn my bread
   And creamless tea,
And wish I wi' the pot was laid
   Low in the clay.

For, ah! I'm sure I'll never see
Such joys as charm'd my youthfu' e'e –
The days are past when folks like me
    Could earn their bread,
My auld wheel now sits silently
    Aboon the bed.

And well may Erin weep and wail
The day the wheels began to fail,
Our tradesmen now can scarce get kail
    Betimes to eat,
In shipfuls they are doomed to sail
    In quest of meat.

For that machine that spins the yarn,
Left us unfit our bread to earn,
O Erin! will you ne'er turn stern
    Against your foe,
When every auld wife can discern
    Your overthrow!

DAVID HERBISON (1800–1880)

Source: *Midnight Musings; or Thoughts from the Loom*,
Belfast, 1848

from MY AIN NATIVE TOUN
[1853]

We then had nae drapers the poor to oppress;
We wove our ain wab and we drank our ain glass,
And aye had a shilling to spend or to spare,
The heart to mak' glad that seemed weary wi' care;
Contented we were when we had in our bag
A very fine score, or a six hundred rag;
Our sweethearts aye met us wi' joy in their face,
Mirth reigned in their pride, and made happy ilk place;
Our coats were hame spun, and our sarks were the
    same,
And warmly we welcomed a frien' whan he came;
Our rent was aye paid whan the rent day came roun'
When I was a boy in my ain native toun.

Until we ceased selling our claith in the hall,
Nae want was amang us our peace to enthrall,
For a' kind o' wark we had plenty o' cash,
And merchants that ne'er cut a bit o' a dash;
They were perfectly honest, kind, friendly, and true,
And knew weel the wark they cam' weekly to do;
But, oh, what a change on a' things has cam' roun'
Since I was a boy in my ain native toun.

'Twas heartsome to see on a Saturday morn,
Before the red clouds o' their tassels were shorn,
Our blithe bonnie lasses come into the toun,
A' tidy and braw in their hame-woven goun;
And heartsome to see the big bunch in their arms,
Of which they were proud as they were o' their
    charms;
And while it was praised, paid, and carried awa,

Their smiles and their glances enlivened us a';
What courting and talking in love we enjoyed
When a' at the wheel and the reel were employed,
Our hearthstanes were cozie, the sang was sang roun',
When I was a boy in my ain native toun.

Oh had I the power the past to restore,
The reel wad still crack, and the spinning-wheel snore,
Mill-yarn wad sink doun as it never had been,
Trade flourish as fair as it ever was seen;
Distress and oppression flee far frae our view,
Our hamlets rejoice and their beauties renew;
The profligate band that brought want to our door
Should labour or starve on a far foreign shore;
A wab in a steamloom should never appear,
Our country to steep in affliction and fear;
Peace, pleasure, and plenty, and happy hearts roun',
And times wad revive in my ain native toun.

DAVID HERBISON

Source: *The Select Works of David Herbison*, Belfast, n.d. [1883]

MY SAILOR BOY

There is beauty in Willie's soft smile –
    There is love in my Willie's blue eye –
And his voice has the ring of the song-bird's in spring,
    And he's straight as the feathery rye.

I know that the wild cherry's bloom
    Took its tint from his brow, that's so fair;

And the nuts of Glendhu, they have borrowed their
   hue
   From my true-lover's clustering hair.

I've found out for myself the fair star
   That the mariner loveth to view;
And through the lone night I watch its pale light,
   For my sailor's eye rests on it too.

And I'll listen the wind of the South,
   As it talks with the leaves on the tree;
For that merry South breeze has come over the seas,
   And I'm sure it has tidings for me.

JAMES McKOWEN (1814–1889)

Source: *The Harp of Erin: A Book of Ballad Poetry and Native Song.
Collected, arranged and annotated by Ralph Varian*, Dublin, 1869

A SONG FOR FEBRUARY

Day in an' day oot on his auld farrant loom,
   Time lengthens the wab o' the past;
Dame Nature steps in like a lamp tae the room,
Hir e'e tae the simmer o' life geein' bloom.
So winter slips by, wi' its mirth an' its gloom,
   As spring is appearin' at last.

The robin gets up an' he lauchs in his glee,
   In view o' the prospect so braw;
Sets his heid tae the side, wi' its feathers agee,
As he spies a bit snaw drop at fit o' the tree,
An' says tae himsel' a'll hae denties tae pree
   By an' by when the splash is awa.

The blackbird keeks oot frae the fog at the broo,
    Gees his neb a bit dicht on a stane;
His eye caught the primrose appearin' in view,
An' the tiny wee violet o' Nature's ain blue;
He sung them a sang o' the auld an' the new –
    A sang we may a' let alane.

The thrush cuff't the leaves 'neath the skep o' the
    bee,
    An' he tirrl't them aside wae a zest;
I maun hurry awa tae rehearsal, quo he,
This work fits the sparrow far better than me;
His sang pleased the ear frae the tap o' the tree
    As he fell intae tune wae the rest.

Thus Nature provides for hir hoose an' hir wanes,
    An' we may rejoice in the plan;
The wren tae the bluebonnet sings his refrain
On causey o' cottier or lordly domain;
The wagtail looks on withoot shade o' disdain,
    May we aye say the same o' the man.

THOMAS GIVEN (1850–1917)

Source: *Poems from College and Country by Three Brothers*,
Belfast, 1900

from A MARCH STORM
IN DIFFERENT WAYS

The March wun whussl't ower the hills,
    Wae loud determined souch,
While bladdin' snaw-showers fil't the rills
    That lead tae mony a shouch.
The auld Pun burn, fou tae the brim,
    By Jenny Wylie's rummelt,
Then creepin' on 'neath hazels dim,
    Into the Maine it tummelt,
            Fou dark that day.

The clouds in darkest ragements flung
    Kept singin' as they went,
But whether Psalm or Hymn they sung
    I didna then tak tent.
The squavin' pine, wae dancin' plume,
    Kept noddin' tae the rushes,
That sheltered grew beneath the broom.
    An' ither weer bushes,
            Unkent that day.

The craw in tattered garb o' black,
    Fierce struggled wae the wun,
Until beneath some shelterin' stack,
    He drappet tae the grun.
There croaking forth its hymn o' praise,
    For food and shelter's proffer,
Wha kens but Him o' Ancient Days,
    Wus well pleased wae its offer
            O' thanks that day.

THOMAS GIVEN

Source: op. cit.

from POETICAL EPISTLE
TAE CULLYBACKEY AULD NUMMER
[MASONIC LODGE]

Auld freen and helper up the hill,
By hamely words frae freedom's quill,
O' those wha doubly get their fill
   O' landlord laws,
True men shall thank you wae a will,
   An' help yer cause.

I watched you weel in years remote,
When bailiffs steered the tenants' boat,
How fearlessly you cast your vote
   On freedom's side;
Amang the first you tossed your coat
   'Gainst cursed pride.

You ne'er cud sympathize wae those
Wha havin' plucked at fortune's rose,
Wad straightway pawn their poorhouse clothes,
   And ape the Tory,
While ilka breath o' wind that blows
   Can sing their story.

Can ony independent man,
Wha guides the plough wae wacket han',
While ill laws curse his native lan'
   In ilka way,
Bow down and serve the landlord clan
   For lickplate pay.

Still let us pride in takin' pert
Wae those wha thole oppression's dert,
Let's gae the twa-faced their dessert,

And shut their mooth.
What though oor speech be sometimes tert,
    We'll tell the truth.

The tenants' war that round us rage,
Should a' oor noble thochts engage,
Until we wipe from freedom's page
    The ills that cover,
The homesteads o' the present age,
    And toss them over.

THOMAS GIVEN

Source: op. cit.

from
THE AULD SCHOOL AT THE PUN'

I hear the auld schule at the pun'
    Is nou aboot tae go,
Replacet by yin on wider grun,
    An' better squaret for show;
But, ah! its builders canna move,
    Mid their deliberations,
The beaten pad an' freenly grove
    O' young associations,
            Doon there yin day.

The palmy days are lang awa'
    Whun Craig keek't through his specs,
An' cud tak' in frae wig tae wa'
    Oor weest pranks an' acts.
Syntax was little thoucht o' then,
    But heth we had tae mind it,

For at the very pointer's en'
   He taught us how tae find it,
      By nicht or day.

Then whun the maister didna see,
   Oor pea guns answer't weel,
Charge't frae a pretae cut in three,
   Stuck in an auld goose queel.
The smirkin' lass wha boun the rest
   Stood nearly head an' shouther,
Was sarely plague't, or mebby bless't,
   Wae oor uncertain pouther,
      In cracks that day.

Some wur bedeck't in corduroy,
   An' sakeless o' a shoe;
But as a rule the barefoot boy
   Wae credit aye got through,
As watch him on a Friday nicht
   While Craig the marks is scannin',
He mostly then cam oot a' richt,
   An' at the head kept stannin'
      O' 'is class that day.

Since then what bitter change has come
   Across the line o' years.
Death finds the quotient o' his sum,
   In spite o' a' oor tears.
The usefu' yins wur mostly ta'en,
   In middle o' their summer;
Some, like mysel', that does remain
   Are hardly fit for lummer
      On ony day.

THOMAS GIVEN

Source: op. cit.

GLOSSARY

Only words that cannot be deduced from the text are included.

a': all
aboon: above
ae: all
agee: astray
ahin, ahint: behind
ain, ainie: own
auld farrant: old-fashioned
ava: at all
awee: a short while
ay: aye
ax: to ask

bairn, bairnie: a child
baith: both
bald: bold
bane: bone
bard, bardie: rural rhymer
bean-strow: bean stalks
bed rid: bedridden
beece: beasts
belyve: by and by
bicker: to run quickly
bield: shelter
bin': bind
birky: clever fellow
birl: whirling round
birrin': whirring noise
bit: small quantity
bladdin': heavy
blae: pale blue
bleeze: blaze
boon, boone: a group of
   harvesters

brace: beam supporting
   mantelpiece
brae: slope of hill
braw, brawly, bra': handsome,
   bravely
breed: bread
brislin': crisped with heat
broo: higher side of ditch
brose: pease-porridge
brung: brought
brunt: burnt
burn, burnie: small stream,
   brook
but and ben: kitchen and back
   room

caff: chaff
callan: a boy
cames: combs
camp: to strive
canavan: bog cotton
cantie: cheerful
caust: cast off
chaeny-mem: woman selling
   delph
chiel: a fellow
churn: harvest ritual of
   cutting of last sheaf
claith: cloth
cleg: horse-fly
clout: a cloth
contra': country
crabbit: short-tempered,
   difficult

crack: to talk, to banter
crawtree: buttercup, crowfoot
creashy, creesht: greasy
crowl: dwarf

daigh: dough
deavin': deafening
deen: done
deil: the devil
denty: dainty
dicht: to wipe lightly
dinglin': rattling
dinlin: tingling
dirl: shrill
dos'd: unsound
douce: gentle
dreeper: draper, cloth buyer
drift: snow
drolls: amusing tales
dub: puddle
duds: rags

e'e: the eye
een: the eyes, evening
elf-shot: under a spell
elson: an awl
enou': enough

fa': fall
fairin': a present
fasher: troublesome blow
fasht: troubled
fause: false
faut: fault
fen: live comfortably
fislin': bustling
fittie-fur, fittie lan: a pair of plough-horses

flysome: flighty
fog: long stems of last year's grass
forret: forward
forth: a small mound
frae: from
freen: friend
freet: supernatural warning
fu': full

gab: mouth
gall: bitterness of spirit
gane: gone, going
gape-seed saw: inquisitive
gars: compells
gash: gap-toothed
gaun: gone
geck't: to look at, critically
gif: if
ging'bread: ginger-bread
glaikit: foolish
glaur: mud
gleg-tongued: sharp-tongued
govels: people wandering stupidly
gowd: gold
gowk: a cuckoo, a fool
graise: grease, butter
granny: a grandmother, the last standing sheaf of corn
greet: to weep
groset: a gooseberry
grun': the ground

ha': hall
hae: have
hale: healthy, whole
hallan: pile of turf just outside the house

haverl: witless

haud a wee: hold a little, bide your time

heckle: board with spikes for dressing flax

het: hot

hind: farm labourer

hings: hangs

hippin' and hoyin': shouting to animals

house-easin': the eaves

hovies: hooves

ilk, ilka: each

ingle: fireside

Italic: Italian

jabs: jobs

jag the flea: to sew minutely

jilts: flighty girls

jirgin': squeaking like a fiddle

Jone: John

kail: cabbage

ken: to know

kepp: to catch

kevels: tosses head

kieve: tub or vat for bleaching

kilt: tucked up

kirn: the churn

know'd: gnawed

kye: cows

lagh: laugh

laigh: low

langsyne: long ago

lave: the remainder

leal: faithful

lear: learning

ledge: declare, assert

libbin': striking with baton

lievin': alive

lift: sky

limber'-bearers: legs

loghter: a handful of corn

loof: palm of the hand

loun: quiet

lowin': flaming

lowtin': crouching

lug: the ear

lum: the chimney

lummer: lumber

mair: more

mashlin': mixed corn

maun: must

menseless: ill-bred

mooth: mouth

muntins: mountains

nae: no, not

naigies: horses

neb: nose, beak

neist: next

nerra-gauge: narrow-gauge railway

Nickie-Ben: friendly name for the devil

nit: nut

noggin: wooden drinking vessel

nybers: neighbours

o': of

oure, ower: over, too

outbye: out of doors

outler: unhoused

pappit: puppet
pay't: paid
pease-strae: pea stalks
pegh: to pant
pense: pence
pike: pole with metal tip or
    blade
plack: a mouthful
Point an' Prataoes: dinner
    without meat, jocular
poortith: poverty
pouther: powder
pratoe, pretae: potato
pree: to taste
pried: tasted
puir hoose: poor house
pun': the pound for
    empounding stray beasts
puts [him]: directs

quat: to quit
queel: a quill
quiltin': joint sewing session

rade: active
rail: corncrake
raildom: the railway station
rais: bottom of old ditches
rant: frolic
rauckle: stout, strong
raw: row
reek: smoke
reest: part of plough
riddle: sieve
rin': run
round: to roll
rowtin: bellowing

rung: club or baton
runkled: wrinkled

sads: depression
sae: so
sair: sore
sakeless: without
salie: salley, willow
sark: shirt, chemise
sauce scobes: willow rods
sauld: sold
scabby get: fledgling
scaur: scare, alarm
scuddin' hoofs: slapping hands
    in bargain
seely: simple, silly
sett: number of rigs to be
    reaped
shamy: disreputable
shankies: legs
shaw: a small wooden hollow
sheugh, shouch: a ditch
    usually with water in it
shilpin: weak, feeble, puny, pale
    and sickly looking
shinny: a game with curved
    sticks
shods: horse shoes
shouther: shoulder
sic: such
skailt: scattered
slae: sloe, blackthorn
sleek: to smooth
slugs: a kind of potato
sma': small
sna', snaw: snow
snell: chilly
snoot-clout: handkerchief
soger: a soldier

sough: sound of wind, sigh
sowens: a dish of boiled
    oatmeal
speel: to climb
spier: to ask
sprigtail: an upstart
spunkie: mettlesome
squagh: to squawk
stead: a bedstead
stifflin': stifling
stitch the louse: fine work
    with a needle
stoge: a stodgy person
stoiter: to stagger, to walk
    carelessly
stoup: a jug or mug
straught: straight
sud: should
suggans: straw ropes
sweel't: wasting away
syne: since, thereafter

targin': scolding fiercely
tent: heed, attention
tert: tart
theek: to thatch
thole: to endure
tift: temper, humour
timmer: timber
tither: the other
travallie: noisy crowd
trimmel: tremble
truckle: small cart
tugs: reins, harness
unco: extraordinary,
    extremely

unkent: unknown

vent: an opening

wa': wall
wacket: hard, calloused
waesucks: woe
waeworth: alas
wakerife: sleepless
wan'erers: wanderers
warl': world
wat: wet
wauk: wake
wean: small child
weer: smaller
wham: whom
whan: when
wheeper: fife
wheezelin': wheezing
whinge: to complain, to whine
whist: be quiet
whye: whey
whyles: at times
wi': with
woodquest: woodpigeon
wun: wound
w'y: way

yads: old mares
yett: a gate
yins: ones
yirth: earth
yockt: yoked

INDEX